THE COMMAND HABIT

Biblical Commands to Follow

A 31-Day Devotional

ILYNMW Publishing
Atlanta Georgia

Books by Paul Beersdorf

Flowers on Tuesday
52 Things I Wish My Father Had Told Me about Marriage
and Family
The 100 Most Important Words
Encouraging Your Wife
Encouraging Your Husband
Advice for Today, Tomorrow and Forever
Even Moses Needed Encouragement
Storm Management
Living Intentionally
Luck, Chance or Prayer
Choosing to Finish Well
Destination – Dad 2.0
Characteristics of a Leader
Unleadership
Character of God – Devotional
Parents, Prodigals and Prayer - Devotional

Table of Contents

Dedication   Page 5
Introduction   Page 6
Choosing to Finish Well   Page 8
Biblical Commands   Page 11

Day 1   Love God   Page 21
Day 2   Love Others   Page 28
Day 3   Rejoice Always   Page 35
Day 4   Pray Without Ceasing   Page 42
Day 5   In All Things Give Thanks   Page 48
Day 6   Take Every Thought Captive   Page 54
Day 7   Make No Provision For The Flesh   Page 60
Day 8   Seek Justice   Page 66
Day 9   Love Mercy   Page 72
Day 10   Walk Humbly with God   Page 78
Day 11   What you Dwell Upon   Page 84
Day 12   Set Your Mind   Page 90
Day 13   Draw Near to God/Abide   Page 96
Day 14   Commit Your Works   Page 102
Day 15   Do Not Become Conformed   Page 108
Day 16   Trust in the Lord   Page 114
Day 17   Be Strong and Courageous   Page 120
Day 18   Keep Free from Love of Money   Page 126
Day 19   Flee Temptation   Page 132
Day 20   Shine Your Light   Page 138
Day 21   Cast Your Burden   Page 144
Day 22   Love One Another   Page 150
Day 23   Choose Who You will Serve   Page 156
Day 24   Continue in God's Word   Page 162
Day 25   Render to Caesar   Page 168
Day 26   Watch and Pray   Page 173
Day 27   Repent   Page 179
Day 28   Love Your Enemies   Page 185
Day 29   Be Reconciled   Page 191
Day 30   Lay-up Treasures   Page 197
Day 31   Make Disciples   Page 203
Epilogue   Page 208
Summary   Page 210
Final Thoughts   Page 222

Dedication

This book is dedicated to my beautiful Bride Debbie!

I love my Beautiful Bride and how much she encourages me to write and share my thoughts and ideas.   She is the love of my life and my best friend.   Nothing I do would be worthwhile without her by my side.

I love you no matter what!
You are the love of my life!
You are my best friend ever seen!
All of me loves all of you!
You are the only one for me!
You are the desire of my heart!
You captivate my heart!
You complete me and make me a better man!
If I had to choose all over again, I would choose you!
Thanks for saying yes!
I choose you!
143

Introduction

The genesis of this book is from a list of scripture that I called my "Daily Bakers Dozen". It consists of 13 different bible scriptures that are "commands" that I want to remember and follow every day.

1. Love God
2. Love Others
3. Rejoice Always
4. Pray Without Ceasing
5. In All Things Give Thanks
6. Take Every Thought Captive
7. Make No Provision For The Flesh
8. Seek Justice
9. Love Mercy
10. Walk Humbly With God
11. Dwell on Pure Thoughts
12. Set Your Mind on Heaven
13. Draw Near To God And Commit To Him

I start my prayer and Bible time each day with these 13 commands (I keep them short – just a few words of the actual scripture), to remind myself how I want to conduct my day. This also ties in with another principle I have each day which is "Choosing to Finish Well". These are seven different aspects of my life where I want to finish well each day.

In memorizing the Daily Bakers Dozen I felt I had a good foundation each day. However, it got me thinking about other Biblical commands and how I should apply those to my life as well. Therefore, I started researching and came up with the idea for this devotional. It is written to myself first (as I need as much study in God's word as I can possibly get), and secondarily to you the reader.

Following is my life verse and the desire I have to strive to live out these verses each and every day (most days still falling short, but striving nonetheless).

I Thessalonians 5:16 - 18

16 Rejoice always;
17 pray without ceasing;
18 in everything give thanks; for this is God's will for you in Christ Jesus.

Blessing to you! I hope you enjoy this devotional.

Choosing to Finish Well

In a previous book I wrote called "Choosing to Finish Well", I talk about the seven areas of life that I wanted to focus upon each day so that I could finish well that day.

As I thought about these seven key areas of my life I wanted to distill this down to one word or phrase for each area. Not only would this make it easier for me to remember, but it would also make it easier for me to share with others. In business we would call this our "elevator speech". In other words, it can be done in about 15-30 seconds.

So here goes – I want to be:

Physically   – FIT
Relationally   – ENGAGED
Economically   – SOUND
Mentally   – POSITIVE
Intellectually   – CURIOUS
Spiritually   – GROUNDED
Emotionally   – SENSITIVE

Note the first letter of these key words spell out the acronym P.R.E.M.I.S.E.

What is a PREMISE? It is a statement taken to be true and used as a basis for argument or reasoning.

Here is one of the more common definitions of a premise that helps people to understand the meaning.

- All humans are mortal.
- The president is a human.
- Therefore, the president is mortal.

So here is my PREMISE

- Choices define how someone will live their life.
- We all have the ability to make choices.
- Therefore, you hold the authority over the shape of your existence through the choices you make.

Biblical commands demand a response—obedience, disobedience, or indifference. I pray you don't just learn these truths, but internalize them, committing yourself to the daily practice of living them out."

We all begin with the intention of finishing well. No one starts a marathon planning to quit at mile thirteen, and no one begins their spiritual journey hoping to become lukewarm, cynical, or distracted. Yet, for many of us, "spiritual drift" is the quiet reality of our lives. We don't usually turn away from our faith in a single, dramatic moment of rebellion; instead, we drift away in a thousand tiny, un-commanded moments.

This book was born out of a simple but transformative realization: **The life you want is hidden in the habits you avoid.**

The Power of the "Command Habit"

In our modern culture, the word "command" often feels heavy, restrictive, or outdated. We prefer words like "suggestions," "intentions," or "preferences." But in the Kingdom of God, commands are not burdens designed to restrict our freedom; they are guardrails designed to protect our joy.

When Jesus said, *"If you love Me, you will keep My commandments"* (John 14:15), He wasn't giving us a checklist for earned merit. He was giving us the logistics for a relationship. He was teaching us that love is not a vague feeling—it is a series of decisive actions that eventually become our second nature.

A "Command Habit" is the point where obedience becomes a reflex. It is the moment when you no longer have to debate whether to be honest, whether to pray, or whether to rejoice, because those actions have been woven into the very fabric of who you are.

Over the next month, we will look at thirty-one specific biblical directives. We will study the lives of "finishers" like **William Tyndale, Fanny Crosby,** and **Brother Lawrence** — people who proved that the "Command Habit" can sustain a soul through fire, blindness, and the mundane clatter of a kitchen.

How to Use This Book

This is not a book to be "read"; it is a book to be "inhabited."

1. **Read the Daily Verse:** Let the Word of God be your North Star for the day.

2. **Ponder the Lessons:** Don't rush through the historical examples or the "Prince of Preachers" insights.

3. **Practice the Habit:** Every day ends with a practical application. Do not skip this. A habit is only formed through the "doing."

4. **Engage the Reflection:** Use the questions to audit your own heart.

A Final Word

The goal of this devotional is not perfection; it is **continuity**. If you miss a day, don't let the enemy use it as a "supply line" for guilt. Simply pick up where you left off. The "Command Habit" is built one day at a time, one choice at a time.

You are not just reading a book; you are building the architecture of a life that will stand when the storms come. You are learning to finish well.

Let's begin.

Biblical Commands

The number of commands in the Bible depends entirely on how you define a "command." Are you looking for ancient legal statutes, grammatical imperatives (verbs that issue an order), or the most famous moral laws?

Because there isn't one "official" list, scholars and theologians categorize them in a few different ways:

1. The Jewish Tradition: 613 Mitzvot

In the Old Testament (specifically the first five books known as the Torah), Jewish tradition identifies **613 commandments**. This count was famously codified by the scholar Maimonides in the 12th century.

- **248 Positive Commandments:** "Thou shalt..." (acts to perform).

- **365 Negative Commandments:** "Thou shalt not..." (acts to avoid).

- **The Ten Commandments:** These are the most well-known, found in Exodus 20 and Deuteronomy 5, and are considered the foundation for the other 603.

2. The New Testament: 1,050 Commands

While the New Testament is often viewed through the lens of "grace" rather than "law," it actually contains a high number of instructions for Christian living.

- **Dake's Count:** One of the most cited counts (from *Dake's Annotated Reference Bible*) identifies **1,050 commands** in the New Testament.

- **Themes:** These range from moral instructions (like "flee from idolatry") to social duties (like "honor the king") and spiritual disciplines (like "pray without ceasing").

3. The Grammatical Count: 1,632 Imperatives

If you look strictly at the original Greek text of the New Testament and count every time a verb is in the **imperative mood** (a direct order), the number is higher.

- Scholar James Boyer identified **1,632 imperatives** in the New Testament.

- However, many of these are situational (e.g., Jesus telling a specific person to "Go and wash") rather than universal moral laws for everyone to follow.

4. Jesus' Summary: The Two Greatest

When Jesus was asked which commandment was the most important, he famously distilled the thousands of biblical instructions down to just **two**:

1. **Love the Lord your God** with all your heart, soul, and mind.

2. **Love your neighbor** as yourself. He stated that "all the Law and the Prophets hang on these two commandments" (Matthew 22:40).

Summary Table

Category	Source	Approx. Count
The Decalogue	Exodus / Deuteronomy	10
Old Testament (Torah)	Jewish Tradition (Mitzvot)	613
New Testament	Dake's List	1,050
New Testament (Grammar)	Greek Imperative Mood	1,632

Total Estimate: If you combine the traditional 613 Old Testament laws with the 1,050 New Testament instructions, there are roughly **1,663 commands** that provide a framework for biblical living.

Now that we have the "accounting" of commands, below is a list of the Biblical commands I have included in this devotional. Based on what you just read, it is obvious that this list is not exhaustive!

However, In my opinion, these are some of the most important commands to follow and certainly, from a practical day to day perspective these are the commands I have focused on in my daily devotional.

The first two – Love God and Love Others – encompass all the commands as Jesus eloquently taught in the New Testament. I am sure true Biblical scholars could create a more impactful and impressive list. However, this is my list and I hope it will be impactful in your life and walk with God.

Love God

You shall love the Lord your God with all your heart and with all your soul and with all your might.
Deuteronomy 6:5

Love Others

" and you shall love the Lord your God with all your heart, and with all your soul, and with all your mind, and with all your strength.' The second is this, 'You shall love your neighbor as yourself.' There is no other commandment greater than these."
Mark 12:30-31

Rejoice Always

Rejoice always; pray without ceasing; in everything give thanks; for this is God's will for you in Christ Jesus.
1 Thessalonians 5:16-18

Pray Without Ceasing

Rejoice always; pray without ceasing; in everything give thanks; for this is God's will for you in Christ Jesus.
1 Thessalonians 5:16-18

In All Things Give Thanks

Rejoice always; pray without ceasing; in everything give thanks; for this is God's will for you in Christ Jesus.
1 Thessalonians 5:16-18

Take Every Thought Captive

We are destroying speculations and every lofty thing raised up against the knowledge of God, and we are taking every thought captive to the obedience of Christ,
 2 Corinthians 10:5

Make No Provision For The Flesh

But put on the Lord Jesus Christ, and make no provision for the flesh in regard to its lusts.
Romans 13:14

Seek Justice

He has told you, O man, what is good;
And what does the Lord require of you
But to do justice, to love mercy,
And to walk humbly with your God?
Micah 6:8

Love Mercy

He has told you, O man, what is good;
And what does the Lord require of you
But to do justice, to love mercy,
And to walk humbly with your God?
Micah 6:8

Walk Humbly with God

He has told you, O man, what is good;
And what does the Lord require of you
But to do justice, to love mercy,
And to walk humbly with your God?
Micah 6:8

What you Dwell Upon

Finally, brethren, whatever is true, whatever is honorable, whatever is right, whatever is pure, whatever is lovely, whatever is of good repute, if there is any excellence and if anything worthy of praise, dwell on these things.
Philippians 4:8

Set Your Mind

Set your mind on the things above, not on the things that are on earth.
Colossians 3:2

Draw Near to God/Abide

Draw near to God and He will draw near to you. Cleanse your hands, you sinners; and purify your hearts, you double-minded.
James 4:8

Commit Your Works

Commit your works to the Lord And your plans will be established.
Proverbs 16:3

Do Not Become Conformed

And do not be conformed to this world, but be transformed by the renewing of your mind, so that you may prove what the will of God is, that which is good and acceptable and perfect.
Romans 12:2

Trust in the Lord

Trust in the Lord with all your heart And do not lean on your own understanding. In all your ways acknowledge Him, And He will make your paths straight.
Proverbs 3:5-6

Be Strong and Courageous

"Be strong and courageous, do not be afraid or tremble at them, for the Lord your God is the one who goes with you. He will not fail you or forsake you."
Deuteronomy 31:6

Keep Free from Love of Money

Make sure that your character is free from the love of money, being content with what you have; for He Himself has said, "I will never desert you, nor will I ever forsake you,"
Hebrews 13:5

Flee Temptation

Now flee from youthful lusts and pursue righteousness, faith, love and peace, with those who call on the Lord from a pure heart.
Timothy 2:22

Shine Your Light

Let your light shine before men in such a way that they may see your good works, and glorify your Father who is in heaven.
Matthew 5:16

Cast Your Burden

Cast your burden upon the Lord and He will sustain you; He will never allow the righteous to be shaken.
Psalm 55:22

Love One Another

A new commandment I give to you, that you love one another, even as I have loved you, that you also love one another.
John 13:34

Choose Who You will Serve

If it is disagreeable in your sight to serve the Lord, choose for yourselves today whom you will serve: whether the gods which your fathers served which were beyond the River, or the gods of the Amorites in whose land you are living; but as for me and my house, we will serve the Lord."
Joshua 24:15

Continue in God's Word

So Jesus was saying to those Jews who had believed Him, "If you continue in My word, then you are truly disciples of Mine; and you will know the truth, and the truth will make you free."
John 8:31-32

Render to Caesar

And Jesus said to them, "Render to Caesar the things that are Caesar's, and to God the things that are God's." And they were amazed at Him.
Mark 12:17

Watch and Pray

In the morning, O Lord, You will hear my voice; In the morning I will order my prayer to You and eagerly watch.
Psalm 5:3

Keep watching and praying that you may not enter into temptation; the spirit is willing, but the flesh is weak."
Matthew 26:41

Repent

From that time Jesus began to preach and say, "Repent, for the kingdom of heaven is at hand."
Matthew 4:17

Love Your Enemies

But I say to you, love your enemies and pray for those who persecute you,
Matthew 5:44

Be Reconciled

Therefore if you are presenting your offering at the altar, and there remember that your brother has something against you, leave your offering there before the altar and go; first be reconciled to your brother, and then come and present your offering.
Matthew 5:23-24

Lay up Treasures

"Do not store up for yourselves treasures on earth, where moth and rust destroy, and where thieves break in and steal. But store up for yourselves treasures in heaven, where neither moth nor rust destroys, and where thieves do not break in or steal; for where your treasure is, there your heart will be also.
Matthew 6:19-21

Make Disciples

Go therefore and make disciples of all the nations, baptizing them in the name of the Father and the Son and the Holy Spirit,
Matthew 28:19

Was there anything on this list that surprised you? Which command resonated with you the most? Which command do you need to adhere to the most right now?

Take a few minutes to stop and pray and thank God for the Bible and the continuing instruction we receive each and every day we choose to study

Blessing to you

Citations and Sources

- **Boyer, James L.** (1987). *"The Classification of Imperatives: A Statistical Study."* Grace Theological Journal. (Source for the 1,632 NT imperatives).

- **Dake, Finis J.** (1963). *Dake's Annotated Reference Bible.* Dake Publishing. (Source for the 1,050 NT commands).

- **Maimonides, Moses.** (12th Century). *Sefer Hamitzvot* (The Book of Commandments). Translated into various editions (e.g., Yale Judaica Series). (Source for the 613 Mitzvot).

- **The Bible (NIV/KJV/ESV).** Specifically Exodus 20, Deuteronomy 5, and Matthew 22:34–40 for the Ten Commandments and the "Greatest" Commandments.

Day 1

Love God!

You shall love the Lord your God with all your heart and with all your soul and with all your might.
Deuteronomy 6:5

This chapter addresses the pinnacle of the biblical commands.

We will discuss the horizontal duties of making disciples (Day 31) and being reconciled (Day 29), however, we will now start with the vertical foundation that makes everything else possible.

This is the command that Jesus called "the great and foremost commandment."

Chapter 1: The Greatest Commandment

Key Verse: *"You shall love the Lord your God with all your heart and with all your soul and with all your might."* — **Deuteronomy 6:5 (NASB)**

The Totality of Devotion

The setting for this verse is the *Shema*, the central declaration of the Jewish faith.

It was the first prayer a Jewish child learned and the last words a martyr whispered. It represents a total-life commitment.

In the original Hebrew, the command uses three distinct words to describe the scope of our love:

1. **Heart (*Lebab*):** This refers to the inner man—the seat of the will, the intellect, and the intentions. To love God with the heart is to choose Him with your mind.

2. **Soul (*Nephesh*):** This refers to your life-force, your breath, and your very being. It is the emotional and physical essence of who you are.

3. **Might (*Me'od*):** This is a fascinating word that literally means "muchness" or "abundance." It implies loving God with all your resources, your influence, and your "extra."

God is not looking for a "piece" of your life or a "slice" of your Sunday. He is looking for a love that saturates every dimension of your existence.

A Lesson from History: Augustine's Ordered Love

Augustine of Hippo, the 4th-century theologian, spent the first half of his life searching for love in all the wrong places.

He pursued intellectual fame, physical pleasure, and social status. Yet, he remained profoundly empty.

His conversion was a radical re-ordering of his loves.

He realized that sin is often just "disordered love"—loving a good thing (like money or career) as if it were the "Ultimate Thing." Augustine taught that we can only truly love our neighbor or ourselves once we have placed our primary love on God.

In his famous *Confessions*, he wrote:

"Thou hast made us for Thyself, O Lord, and our heart is restless until it finds its rest in Thee."

Augustine finished well because he stopped trying to fill a "God-shaped hole" with earthly things and began to "render" his entire being to the Creator.

The Compass of the Soul

Love for God acts as the "true north" on the compass of your life.

When a compass is working correctly, the needle always returns to the north, no matter how much you shake the device.

In the same way, when you love God with all your "might," your decisions naturally align with His will. When you face a financial choice, your love for God guides your spending. When you face a conflict, your love for God guides your response.

Loving God is not just an emotion; it is a gravitational pull that keeps your life in orbit.

The Story of the Two Sailors

Imagine two sailors on a dark night. One sailor looks down at the waves, trying to navigate by the movement of the water. But, because the water is always changing, he quickly becomes lost and crashes into the rocks.

The second sailor looks up at the North Star. The star is always fixed and unchanging. By keeping his eyes on the star, he can easily navigate through the roughest seas and arrive safely at his intended destination.

To love God is to keep your eyes on the "Fixed Star." The waves of culture and the winds of circumstance will change, but the character of God remains the same. If He is your "Greatest Love," you will always know which way to turn.

Wisdom from a "Man of Science"

Blaise Pascal, the brilliant 17th-century mathematician and physicist, realized that the human mind could never satisfy the human heart.

Despite his massive contributions to science, he found his ultimate purpose in the "fire" of God's love.

Pascal noted:

"There is a God-shaped vacuum in the heart of each man which cannot be satisfied by any created thing but only by God the Creator."

Pascal understood that loving God was the only rational response to the reality of our design. He saw that without this primary love, all other achievements were merely "rust and moth".

How to "Love God" Today

Loving God is a practice, not just a feeling. Here is how you can apply Deuteronomy 6:5 this week:

1. **The "Me'od" Audit:** Look at your "muchness"—your extra time, your extra money, and your specific talents. How can you use your "abundance" to show love to God this week? Or better yet, how can you show the love of God to others with your muchness?

2. **The Mindful Morning:** as you begin your day, simply spend two minutes telling God why you love Him. Focus on His attributes: His holiness, His mercy, His constancy.

3. **The Obedience Connection:** Jesus said, "If you love Me, you will keep My commandments" (**John 14:15**). Identify one command you have been neglecting and follow it today as an "act of love."

For the Christian, our greatest "victory" is the daily triumph of choosing to love God over our own selfish desires.

A Moment for Reflection

Is God the "Sun" of your universe, or just another "planet" revolving around you?

We often want to be the center of the Universe and just ask God do our bidding and to bless our plans, protect our "treasures," and help our "disciples," while we keep ourselves as the center of the universe and unwilling to change our trajectory.

Deuteronomy 6:5 is a call to "flee" from the idolatry of self. It is an invitation to be part of something bigger than your own story.

Today, look at the "muchness" of your life. Turn your compass toward the North Star. Give Him your heart, your soul, and your might — and watch how everything else in your life finally finds its proper place.

Closing Prayer

Lord, I thank You that You loved me first. I confess that my heart is often divided, and I give my "might" to things that do not last. Please re-order my loves today. Help me to love You with every fiber of my being and every resource at my disposal. May my life be a continuous song of devotion to You. Amen.

Reflection & Action: The Triple-Threat Love

1. **Auditing Your "Muchness":** The Hebrew word for "might" (*me'od*) literally means your "muchness" or abundance. Looking at your current life — your extra time, your specific professional skills, or your financial surplus — how much of your "abundance" is being used to further God's Kingdom versus simply increasing your own earthly comfort?

2. **The Compass Test:** When a crisis "shakes the compass" of your life, does your internal needle eventually return to God as its True North, or do you find yourself navigating by the "waves" of your emotions or the opinions of others? What is one specific situation right now where you need to stop looking at the waves and look back at the Star?

3. **Identifying Disordered Loves:** Augustine taught that sin is often just "disordered love" — treating a good thing (like your family, your reputation, or your health) as if it were the *Ultimate Thing*. If you look at your recent anxieties, do they reveal a "good thing" that has accidentally moved into the central throne of your heart?

4. **Beyond the Intellectual:** Loving God with the "soul" (*nephesh*) involves our inner self and emotions. Is your devotion to God currently characterized more by a cold, intellectual "heart" agreement, or does it actually permeate your "soul" — the way you breathe, feel, and react to the world around you? How can you move from merely *studying* Him to truly *delighting* in Him this week?

Reflection

Take a few minutes to reflect and meditate on what you just read. Write
down your thoughts take time to pray and praise God.

_____

_____

_____

_____

_____

_____

_____

_____

_____

_____

_____

_____

_____

_____

_____

_____

References and Further Reading

- **Augustine's "Confessions":**
  https://www.gutenberg.org/files/3296/3296-h/3296-h.htm

- **Word Study: Me'od (Might/Muchness):**
  https://www.blueletterbible.org/lexicon/h3966/nasb95/wlc/0-1/

- **Pascal's "Pensees" on the God-Shaped Vacuum:**
  https://www.ccel.org/ccel/pascal/pensees.html

- **The Shema in Jewish Tradition:**
  https://www.myjewishlearning.com/article/the-shema/

Day 2

Love Others

" and you shall love the Lord your God with all your heart, and with all your soul, and with all your mind, and with all your strength.' The second is this, 'You shall love your neighbor as yourself.' There is no other commandment greater than these."
Mark 12:30-31

This chapter explores the essential companion to the Greatest Commandment. On Day 1, we looked at the vertical requirement to love God with everything we are. Now, Jesus explains that this vertical love must have a horizontal expression. To love the Creator while ignoring those created in His image is a spiritual impossibility.

Chapter 2: The Inseparable Command

Key Verse: *"'And you shall love the Lord your God with all your heart, and with all your soul, and with all your mind, and with all your strength.' The second is this, 'You shall love your neighbor as yourself.' There is no other commandment greater than these."* — **Mark 12:30-31 (NASB)**

The Two-Fold Law

When Jesus was asked which commandment was the most important, He gave a two-part answer.

He tied the ancient *Shema* (Deuteronomy 6:5) to a command from Leviticus 19:18: "Love your neighbor as yourself." By linking them, Jesus showed that these are not two separate options, but two sides of the same coin.

The word for "neighbor" in the original Greek is *plēsion*, which literally means "the one who is near." It doesn't just refer to the person living in the house next to yours; it refers to whoever God has placed in your path at any given moment.

To "love" them (*agapē*) is to actively seek their well-being with the same intensity and instinctive care that you use to provide for your own needs.

A Lesson from History: William Booth's One-Word Telegram

General William Booth, the founder of The Salvation Army, was a man who understood that loving God was inseparable from serving the "submerged tenth" of society — the homeless, the addicted, and the outcasts of Victorian London.

At the end of his life, when he was too ill to attend the annual Salvation Army convention, he wanted to send a telegram to the delegates to encourage them.

Because telegrams were charged by the word and the organization was always short on funds, he chose to be as brief as possible. He sent a message containing only one word:

"OTHERS."

Booth realized that the secret to finishing well — and the ultimate expression of our faith — is the shift from self-interest to "others-interest."

He spent his life "rendering" his strength to those who could give him nothing in return, because he saw the image of God in every face on the street.

The Mirror of Love

Imagine a mirror. A mirror has no light of its own. Its only purpose is to catch the light from a source—like the sun—and reflect it into the dark corners of a room.

Our love for others is the reflection of God's love for us.

If we are not loving those around us, it is a sign that we have turned away from the Source. We don't "generate" the love ourselves; we simply position ourselves to catch God's *agapē* and redirect it toward our "neighbor."

If the mirror is covered in the "dust" of selfishness or bitterness, the light cannot bounce off us to help anyone else see.

The Standard of Self-Love

Jesus provides a very practical yardstick for this command: "as yourself."

Think about how much effort you put into your own life. When you are hungry, you find food. When you are cold, you find a coat. When you are insulted, you defend your reputation.

Jesus is asking us to take that same level of "alertness" and apply it to the people around us.

If you see a neighbor who is "hungry" for encouragement, "feed" them. If you see someone "cold" from isolation, "clothe" them with your presence. The command is to treat their needs with the same urgency as our own.

Wisdom from a "Common-Sense" Theologian

C.S. Lewis, the great 20th-century author and scholar, wrote extensively about the practical nature of Christian love. He cautioned against waiting for a "feeling" of love before acting.

Lewis wrote in *Mere Christianity*:

"Do not waste time bothering whether you 'love' your neighbor; act as if you did. As soon as we do this we find one of the great secrets. When you are behaving as if you loved someone, you will presently come to love them."

Lewis understood that *agapē* is a muscle. The more you use it to serve others, the stronger the "feeling" becomes.

How to "Love Others" Today

Loving your neighbor is a series of intentional choices made throughout the day.

1. **The "Plēsion" Awareness:** As you go through your day, consciously identify who your "neighbor" is in each moment—the cashier, the coworker, the person in the car next to you. Remind yourself: "This person is God's property; how can I love them right now?"

2. **The Self-Check Mirror:** When you are about to make a decision, ask: "If I were in their shoes, what would I want someone to do for me?" (The Golden Rule).

3. **The "Others" Prayer:** In your "Watch and Pray", don't just pray for your own needs. Specifically ask God: "Lord, show me one person today whose burden I can help carry."

As the great educator Horace Mann said:

"Doing nothing for others is the undoing of ourselves."

When we refuse to love others, we wither spiritually. When we pour ourselves out, we find that God continuously refills our "well."

A Moment for Reflection

Who is the "neighbor" you find most difficult to love? Is it because they are different from you, or because they have "something against you"?

Remember that Jesus did not say, "Love your neighbor if they are likable."

He said to love them as you love yourself—with a persistent, active commitment to their good.

Today, pick one person you have been ignoring or avoiding and find one "beautiful work" you can do for them. Take the "mirror" of your life and tilt it toward them.

Closing Prayer

Lord, I thank You for the incredible love You have shown me. I confess that I am often so focused on my own needs and my own "treasures" that I fail to see the neighbors You have placed in my path. Please give me Your eyes to see people as You see them. Help me to love with my actions even when my feelings are not there. Use my life to reflect Your light into the dark places of someone else's world. Amen.

Reflection & Action: The Inseparable Love

1. **The Mirror Check:** If your love for others is meant to be a reflection of God's love for you, what does the "quality of the reflection" say about your current connection to the Source? Are you trying to generate kindness out of your own limited patience, or are you consciously drawing from God's infinite grace before interacting with difficult people?

2. **Defining Your "Neighbor":** In the Greek, *plēsion* simply means "the one who is near." Looking at your typical Tuesday—at the grocery store, in traffic, or in the office breakroom—who are the neighbors you have been treating as "background characters" in your story rather than as individuals created in the image of God?

3. **The Self-Care Standard:** Jesus commands you to love your neighbor *as yourself.* We are often very quick to forgive our own mistakes, feed our own hunger, and protect our own reputations. In what specific area of your life can you take the energy you usually spend on your own "well-being" and redirect it toward someone else's this week?

4. **Action Over Emotion:** Recalling C.S. Lewis's advice, is there someone in your life you find difficult to "feel" love for? What would it look like to ignore your feelings for a moment and "act as if" you loved them? How might a simple act of service toward them change the spiritual temperature of your own heart?

Reflection

Take a few minutes to reflect and meditate on what you just read. Write down your thoughts take time to pray and praise God.

_____

_____

_____

_____

_____

_____

_____

_____

_____

_____

_____

_____

_____

_____

_____

_____

_____

_____

_____

References and Further Reading

- **The Life and Legacy of William Booth:**
  https://www.salvationarmy.org.uk/about-us/our-history/our-founders

- **Word Study: Plēsion (Neighbor):**
  https://biblehub.com/greek/4139.htm

- **C.S. Lewis on "The Law of Love":**
  https://www.cslewis.com/tag/love/

Day 3

Rejoice Always

Rejoice always; pray without ceasing; in everything give thanks; for this is God's will for you in Christ Jesus.
1 Thessalonians 5:16-18

This chapter addresses the shortest command in the Greek New Testament, yet it is often the most difficult to maintain. Having established the foundation of loving God (Day 1) and loving others (Day 2), Paul provides a directive that defines the internal atmosphere of the believer.

This is not a suggestion based on our circumstances, but a discipline based on our position in Christ.

Chapter 3: The Choice of Joy

Key Verse: *"Rejoice always."* — **1 Thessalonians 5:16 (NASB)**

The Imperative of Joy

The word "rejoice" in Greek is *chairete*.

It is in the imperative mood, meaning it is a command.

In the mind of the Apostle Paul, rejoicing is not an emotional response to favorable events; it is a spiritual duty. This command is particularly striking because of the word that follows it: **"always."**

Paul was writing to a young church in Thessalonica that was facing significant persecution and social pressure.

He wasn't telling them to be "happy" about their suffering, but to "rejoice" in their Savior. There is a critical distinction between *happiness* and *joy*.

- **Happiness** (from the Old English *hap*) depends on "happenings." If things go well, you are happy.

- **Joy** (*chara*) is a fruit of the Spirit that remains constant regardless of external conditions.

A Lesson from History: Fanny Crosby's "Blessed Assurance"

To understand what it means to "rejoice always," we look at the life of Fanny Crosby.

Blinded by a medical mistake at six weeks old, she lived over 90 years in physical darkness. By the world's standards, she had every reason to be bitter or "unhappy."

Instead, Crosby became the most prolific hymn writer in history, penning over 8,000 hymns including "Blessed Assurance" and "To God Be the Glory."

She viewed her blindness as a gift, once saying that if she were offered her sight, she would refuse it, because "when I get to heaven, the first face that shall ever gladden my sight will be that of my Savior."

She chose to "rejoice always" not because she could see the world, but because she could "see" the truth of the Word, she moved her "treasure" to a place where blindness could not touch it.

The Thermostat vs. The Thermometer

In the spiritual life, you are called to be a thermostat, not a thermometer.

- A **thermometer** merely reflects the temperature of the room. If the environment is cold, the thermometer drops. If the world is angry, the thermometer rises.

- A **thermostat** sets the temperature of the room. It has an internal standard that it maintains regardless of the "weather" outside.

To "rejoice always" is to set your internal spiritual temperature to the joy of the Lord.

When the "chilly winds" of hardship blow, the thermostat of your soul kicks in, drawing heat from the presence of God to maintain a constant state of rejoicing.

The Power of Perspective

Rejoicing is the act of "ordering" your mind to focus on what you have in Christ rather than what you lack in the world.

When you think about mental discipline, the brain cannot easily hold two conflicting emotions at once. When you intentionally practice rejoicing, you are effectively "evicting" anxiety and bitterness from your mental space.

Wisdom from the "Prince of Preachers"

Charles Spurgeon, who struggled with deep bouts of physical pain and depression, spoke often about the "duty" of joy.

He once remarked:

"The joy of the Lord is the best medicine for the soul. It is a Christian's duty to be as happy as he can be, that he may recommend his religion to others."

Spurgeon taught that a joyless Christian is a poor advertisement for a "Great Savior."

He believed that by "continuing" in the promises of God, the believer could find a spring of joy that never runs dry, even in the "desert" of affliction.

How to "Rejoice Always" Today

Rejoicing is a habit of the heart that must be practiced daily.

1. **The "But God" Reframe:** When you face a negative situation today, acknowledge the fact but add the "Rejoice" factor. (Example: "I am stuck in traffic, *but God* is in control of my time and I am grateful for this moment of quiet.")

2. **The Gratitude Inventory:** In your "Morning Watch", list three things that cannot be taken away from you (your salvation, God's presence, the promise of heaven). Rejoice in those specific, "rust-proof" treasures.

3. **The Expression of Joy:** Joy often follows action. Sing a hymn, offer a word of encouragement to a "neighbor", or simply smile. As C.S. Lewis noted, acting as if you have the joy often leads to the reality of the joy.

One of the greatest victories you can win is the victory over your own circumstances by maintaining a heart of joy in a cynical world.

A Moment for Reflection

Are you waiting for your circumstances to change before you decide to be joyful? If so, you will spend your life as a "thermometer," constantly rising and falling with the world's whims.

Jesus said His joy was meant to be "in you" so that your joy "may be full" (**John 15:11**). This fullness doesn't come from a perfect life; it comes from a perfect Savior.

Today, look past the "waves" and fix your eyes on the Source of your joy. Make the choice to "rejoice always" — not because life is easy, but because God is good.

Closing Prayer

Lord, I thank You that You are the source of a joy that the world can neither give nor take away. I confess that I often allow my circumstances to dictate my spirit. Please forgive me for my grumbling and my joylessness. Help me to "set my thermostat" to Your truth today. May Your joy be my strength as I seek to finish well. Amen.

Reflection & Action: The Thermostat of the Soul

1. **Happiness vs. Joy:** Reflect on the last seven days. How many of your "highs" and "lows" were dependent on things you cannot control (traffic, the weather, the opinions of others)? If those external factors were removed, what would remain as the "floor" of your joy?

2. **Setting the Temperature:** In your home or workplace, are you acting as a **thermometer** (merely reflecting the stress or negativity of the room) or a **thermostat** (introducing the joy of Christ to change the atmosphere)? What is one specific "cold" environment in your life that needs you to turn up the spiritual heat this week?

3. **The "Always" Reality:** Paul commands us to rejoice *always*. Identify a "dark room" in your life right now—a situation that feels devoid of happiness. Without ignoring the pain, can you identify one "rust-proof" truth about God (His presence, His promise, or His character) that gives you a reason to rejoice even there?

4. **The Fanny Crosby Perspective:** Fanny Crosby viewed her blindness as a tool that focused her vision on Christ. Is there a "limitation" or "disability" in your life that you have been grieving? How might that very limitation be an invitation to see the face of your Savior more clearly?

Reflection

Take a few minutes to reflect and meditate on what you just read. Write down your thoughts take time to pray and praise God.

_____

_____

_____

_____

_____

_____

_____

_____

_____

_____

_____

_____

_____

_____

_____

_____

References and Further Reading

- **The Life and Hymns of Fanny Crosby:**
  https://www.christianitytoday.com/history/people/poets/fanny
  -crosby.html

- **Word Study: Chairete (Rejoice):**
  https://biblehub.com/greek/5463.htm

- **Spurgeon's "The Joy of the Lord" Sermon:**
  https://www.spurgeon.org/resource-library/sermons/the-joy-of-
  the-lord-is-your-strength/

Day 4

Pray without Ceasing

Rejoice always; pray without ceasing; in everything give thanks; for this is God's will for you in Christ Jesus.
1 Thessalonians 5:16-18

This chapter addresses the practice of constant communion with the Divine. After learning to "rejoice always" (Chapter 3), we now look at the mechanism that sustains that joy. Paul provides a command that, at first glance, seems physically impossible, but when understood through the lens of spiritual posture, it becomes the secret to a life of peace and power.

Chapter 4: The Unbroken Connection

Key Verse: *"Pray without ceasing."* — **1 Thessalonians 5:17 (NASB)**

The Frequency of the Spirit

The command to "pray without ceasing" often confuses the modern reader. We wonder, "How can I work, sleep, or hold a conversation if I am supposed to be praying every second?" The answer lies in the Greek word *adialeiptōs*.

In the ancient world, this word was used to describe a "hacking cough" or a recurring fever.

It didn't mean the person was coughing every single second without a break; it meant the cough was *persistent* and *continual*. It was a condition that stayed with them throughout the day.

To pray without ceasing is to maintain an open line of communication with God.

It is less about the "act" of prayer (the specific words we say) and more about the "atmosphere" of prayer (the awareness of God's presence). It is living in such a way that there is no "hang up" button on your conversation with the Father.

A Lesson from History: Brother Lawrence in the Kitchen

The most famous historical example of this discipline is Nicholas Herman, known as Brother Lawrence, a 17th-century lay monk.

Lawrence was not a high-ranking theologian; he was a humble cook in a monastery kitchen.

While others felt that prayer could only happen in the quiet of a chapel, Lawrence practiced what he called "The Presence of God" amidst the clatter of pots and pans.

He believed that he was just as close to God while washing dishes as he was when kneeling at the altar. He famously said:

"The time of business does not with me differ from the time of prayer; and in the noise and clatter of my kitchen... I possess God in as great tranquility as if I were upon my knees at the blessed sacrament."

Lawrence finished well because he refused to divide his life into "sacred" and "secular" compartments. He understood that 1 Thessalonians 5:17 was an invitation to turn every task into a conversation.

Spiritual Breathing

Theologians often compare unceasing prayer to physical breathing. You do not have to think about breathing for it to happen; it is a background rhythm that sustains your life. You "exhale" your worries, your sins, and your stresses to God, and you "inhale" His peace, His wisdom, and His strength.

If you stop breathing, you die. If you stop the rhythm of prayer, your spiritual life begins to suffocate. "Praying without ceasing" is simply the act of keeping your spiritual lungs open.

The Background "Dial Tone"

Imagine a phone line that is always open.

Even when you aren't speaking, the connection is live. You can whisper a request, shout a "Thank You", or simply listen for the "still small voice" at any moment.

When we "cease" to pray, it is as if we have intentionally cut the wire. We then spend our lives trying to fix our own problems in our own strength, wondering why we feel so disconnected.

Wisdom from the "Prince of Preachers"

Charles Spurgeon believed that unceasing prayer was the hallmark of a mature believer. He noted that we should be in a "praying frame of mind" at all times.

He once remarked:

"Prayer should be the key of the day and the lock of the night. It should be the all-pervading spirit of the entire day."

Spurgeon emphasized that we don't need to be in a specific building or posture to pray.

Whether you are walking down a busy street or sitting in a board meeting, your heart can be "at the throne" while your hands are at work.

How to "Pray Without Ceasing" Today

This discipline turns your ordinary day into an extraordinary walk with God.

1. **The "Breath" Prayer:** Choose a short, one-sentence prayer that you can repeat throughout the day during transitions (getting in the car, waiting for a meeting to start). Examples: "Lord, have mercy," or "Father, I trust You."

2. **The Task-Turning:** Like Brother Lawrence, dedicate your mundane tasks to God. As you fold laundry or write a report, say, "Lord, I do this for Your glory." This keeps the connection "live."

3. **The Immediate Response:** When a worry enters your mind, don't dwell on it for ten minutes before praying. Make the prayer the *first* response. Turn the worry into a "whisper" to the Father immediately.

By weaving threads of prayer throughout your day, you create a "cable" of connection that can withstand any storm.

A Moment for Reflection

Do you only talk to God during "scheduled" times, or is He your constant companion?

Are there areas of your life — your entertainment, your finances, your secret thoughts — where you have "hung up the phone"?

"Praying without ceasing" is not a burden; it is a privilege.

It means you are never alone. You have the Creator of the Universe available for consultation 24 hours a day.

Today, don't "close" your morning prayer. Keep the line open. Take Him with you into the kitchen, the office, and the commute.

Closing Prayer

Lord, I thank You that You are always listening and that Your ear is never heavy. I confess that I often try to live my life in "airplane mode," disconnected from Your presence. Please help me to develop the habit of unceasing prayer. Let my life be a continuous conversation with You, whether I am in the quiet of my room or the noise of the world. Amen.

References and Further Reading

- **Brother Lawrence's "The Practice of the Presence of God":**
  https://www.gutenberg.org/files/5657/5657-h/5657-h.htm

- **Word Study: Adialeiptōs (Unceasingly):**
  https://biblehub.com/greek/82.htm

- **Spurgeon on "Constant Prayer":**
  https://www.spurgeon.org/resource-library/sermons/constant-prayer/

Reflection

Take a few minutes to reflect and meditate on what you just read. Write down your thoughts take time to pray and praise God.

_____

_____

_____

_____

_____

_____

_____

_____

_____

_____

_____

_____

_____

_____

_____

_____

_____

Day 5

Give Thanks

Rejoice always; pray without ceasing; in everything give thanks; for this is God's will for you in Christ Jesus.
1 Thessalonians 5:16-18

This chapter completes the "triad" of commands found in the closing of Paul's first letter to the Thessalonians. We have been commanded to "rejoice always" (Day 3) and "pray without ceasing" (Day 4). Now, we come to the practical expression that seals our joy and sustains our prayer: the discipline of gratitude.

Chapter 5: The Habit of Gratitude

Key Verse: *"In everything give thanks; for this is the will of God in Christ Jesus for you."* — **1 Thessalonians 5:18 (NASB)**

The "In" vs. "For" Distinction

The command in 1 Thessalonians 5:18 is one of the most frequently quoted, yet most frequently misunderstood, verses in the New Testament.

Notice carefully that Paul does not say "give thanks *for* everything." He says, "**in** everything give thanks."

The Greek word for "give thanks" is *eucharisteite*. It is the root from which we get the word "Eucharist." It is built from two smaller words: *eu* (good) and *charis* (grace). Gratitude is the act of recognizing the "good grace" of God even when the "circumstances" of life are difficult.

God does not expect us to be thankful *for* evil, *for* pain, or *for* loss.

However, He commands us to be thankful *in the midst* of those things, because His character and His promises remain unchanged. Gratitude is the spiritual lens that allows us to see the "grace" behind the "grief."

A Lesson from History: Corrie ten Boom and the Fleas

One of the most powerful examples of this "in everything" gratitude comes from the Ravensbrück concentration camp during World War II.

Corrie ten Boom and her sister, Betsie, were imprisoned for hiding Jews from the Nazis. Their barracks were overcrowded, filthy, and — worst of all — infested with fleas.

Betsie insisted they read 1 Thessalonians 5:18 and give thanks for the fleas.

Corrie thought this was ridiculous, but she obeyed. Only later did they discover why the fleas were a "grace." Because of the infestation, the German guards refused to enter their barracks to conduct searches. This allowed the sisters to hold secret Bible studies and bring hope to hundreds of women without interference.

Corrie learned that the very thing she hated was the very thing God was using for her protection. She finished well because she learned to look for the "fountain of grace" in the "valley of fleas."

Greenhouse of the Soul

Gratitude acts like a spiritual greenhouse.

Outside, the world may be freezing, cynical, and harsh. But inside the "glass" of a thankful heart, the environment is controlled.

When we give thanks, we are trapping the "warmth" of God's past faithfulness inside our current situation. This allows the fruit of the Spirit — like joy and peace — to grow even when the "season" of our life should be barren. Without gratitude, our hearts become "frostbitten" by the complaints and murmurs of the culture around us.

The Four-Fold Prayer of Matthew Henry

The great Bible commentator Matthew Henry provides a legendary example of "ordered" gratitude. One day, he was accosted by thieves and robbed of his purse. That night, he wrote in his diary:

"Let me be thankful: First, because I was never robbed before; second, because although they took my purse, they did not take my life; third, because although they took my all, it was not much; and fourth, because it was I who was robbed, not I who robbed."

Henry understood that even in a "bad event," there are multiple layers of "good grace" if we have the eyes to see them. He was practicing the "Render" principle (Chapter 25) by returning praise to God even when the world had taken his money.

Wisdom from the "Prince of Preachers"

Charles Spurgeon believed that gratitude was the "parent" of all other virtues. He noted that a man who is truly thankful to God will find it very difficult to be arrogant, greedy, or bitter.

He once said:

"Give me a thankful heart and I will find in it a thousand reasons for joy. But give me a murmuring heart and I will find in it a thousand reasons for despair."

Spurgeon taught that we should "bless God for the sun, and if He sends the rain, bless Him for that, too; for the one makes the fruit to grow and the other makes the roots to strike deep."

How to "Give Thanks" Today

Gratitude is a muscle that must be exercised until it becomes a reflex.

1. **The "In Everything" Pivot:** The next time something goes wrong today (a spilled coffee, a missed deadline, a rude comment), pause and find one "in" reason to be thankful. (Example: "I am frustrated by this delay, *in* which I am thankful for God's patience with me.")

2. **The Gratitude Journal:** As I mentioned in the "Next Steps" of previous chapters, a journal is vital. Every night this week, write down three specific things from your day that were "grace gifts" from God.

3. **The Vocal Blessing:** Don't just "feel" thankful; say it. Tell someone else what you are grateful for. Gratitude expressed to others is a form of "loving your neighbor" (Chapter 2).

When you choose the "color" of gratitude, the world — even the dark parts of it — begins to look like a canvas for God's grace.

A Moment for Reflection

Is your life characterized by a "sacred silence" of gratitude or the "noisy clatter" of complaints? We often think we will be thankful *after* the problem is solved, but God calls us to be thankful *while* the problem is happening.

Gratitude is the "will of God for you." It is the way you stay aligned with His heart. Today, don't wait for a "flealess" life to be happy. Look at the fleas, look at the "robber," and look at the "rain," and find the *charis* (grace) that is always present.

Closing Prayer

Lord, I thank You that Your mercies are new every morning. I confess that I am prone to grumbling and quick to forget Your past faithfulness. Please give me the eyes of Betsie ten Boom and Matthew Henry. Help me to give thanks "in everything" today, knowing that You are working all things together for my good. May my heart be a greenhouse of Your grace. Amen.

References and Further Reading

- **The Story of Corrie ten Boom:** https://www.tenboom.org/about-corrie-ten-boom/

- **Word Study: Eucharisteo (Give Thanks):**
  https://biblehub.com/greek/2168.htm

- **Spurgeon on "The Duty of Gratitude":**
  https://www.spurgeon.org/resource-library/sermons/the-duty-of-giving-thanks/

Reflection

Take a few minutes to reflect and meditate on what you just read. Write down your thoughts take time to pray and praise God.

_____

_____

_____

_____

_____

_____

_____

_____

_____

_____

_____

_____

_____

_____

_____

_____

_____

_____

Day 6

Capture

We are destroying speculations and every lofty thing raised up against the knowledge of God, and we are taking every thought captive to the obedience of Christ, 2 Corinthians 10:5

This chapter addresses the internal frontier of spiritual warfare. We turn our focus to the "command center" of the human experience: the mind. Paul uses intense military language to describe how a believer must handle the persistent influx of rogue thoughts and false arguments.

Chapter 6: The Battle for the Mind

Key Verse: *"We are destroying speculations and every lofty thing raised up against the knowledge of God, and we are taking every thought captive to the obedience of Christ."* — **2 Corinthians 10:5 (NASB)**

The Prisoner of War

The word Paul uses for "taking captive" is *aichmalotizō.* In the ancient Greco-Roman world, this was a specific military term used to describe the act of leading a prisoner away at spear point after a battle. It implies a total loss of liberty for the captive.

Paul is not suggesting that we merely "ignore" bad thoughts; he is commanding us to arrest them. He views the mind as a battlefield where "speculations" (*logismos* — reasoning's or arguments) and "lofty things" (prideful obstacles) set up fortresses against the truth of God. To finish well, we must become the masters of our mental "prisoners" rather than their servants.

A Lesson from History: John Bunyan's "The Holy War"

John Bunyan, the 17th-century author of *The Pilgrim's Progress*, wrote another profound allegory titled *The Holy War*. In it, he describes the human soul as a city named "Mansoul." The city has five gates: Eye-gate, Ear-gate, Mouth-gate, Feel-gate, and Nose-gate.

Bunyan describes how the enemy, Diabolus, attempts to take the city by sending "doubters" and "false arguments" through the gates to influence the mind. The hero of the story, Prince Emmanuel, teaches the citizens that they must guard the gates and "capture" every intruder.

Bunyan understood from his own years of imprisonment that the true battle is not against physical walls, but against the "strongholds" of the mind.

He finished well — writing masterpieces from a damp prison cell — because he had learned to take his thoughts captive to the peace of Christ, refusing to let the "doubters" of his circumstances take over the city of his soul.

The Fortress of Speculation

We often build "mental fortresses" made of:

- **"What ifs" (Anxiety):** Speculations about a future that hasn't happened.

- **"If onlys" (Regret):** Lofty arguments about a past that cannot be changed.

- **"They think" (Insecurity):** Speculations about the opinions of others (Chapter 26).

These thoughts set themselves up as "higher" than the knowledge of God. When we take a thought "captive," we are essentially bringing it to the "judge" (the Word of God) and asking, "Does this thought obey Christ?" If the thought says "God doesn't love you," and the Word says "I have loved you with an everlasting love," the thought must be arrested and removed from the city.

The 10-Second Rule

In military strategy, a "breach" in the wall must be addressed immediately before the enemy can pour through. The same is true in the mind.

If a rogue thought (bitterness, lust, or fear) is allowed to dwell in the mind for more than a few seconds, it begins to "dig in" and build a stronghold. Taking a thought captive requires an immediate, decisive action the moment it enters the "Eye-gate" or "Ear-gate."

Don't let 10 seconds pass before you take action!

Wisdom from the "Prince of Preachers"

Charles Spurgeon believed that the mind was the "workshop of the soul," and a messy workshop led to a messy life.

He once remarked:

"Our thoughts are the seeds of our acts. If we allow the enemy to sow weeds in our minds, we cannot expect to harvest wheat in our lives."

Spurgeon taught that we should treat a rogue thought like a "spy in the camp." We don't negotiate with it; we don't try to "understand" it; we arrest it and bring it into the light of Christ's obedience.

How to "Capture" Today

This is a high-alert discipline that requires constant vigilance (Chapter 19).

1. **The Mental Gatekeeper:** Throughout the day, ask yourself: "Is this thought a friend of God or an enemy?" If it's an enemy, visualize yourself leading it away at spear point.

2. **The Truth Counter-Attack:** You cannot just "empty" your mind of a bad thought; you must replace it. When you capture a lie, immediately quote a verse of truth (The "Romans Road" mentioned in your premise).

3. **The "Lofty Thing" Demolition:** Identify one recurring "speculation" (like a specific worry or a grudge). Deliberately

"destroy" it by writing it down and then writing the Word of God over it.

When you capture your thoughts, you are choosing to paint your world with the colors of God's truth rather than the "grey" of human speculation.

A Moment for Reflection

Who is the general in charge of your mind today? Are your thoughts running wild, building fortresses of fear and pride, or are they under the strict "obedience of Christ"?

Taking thoughts captive is hard work. It requires more "might" than almost any other discipline. But it is the only way to find true peace. Today, stand at the gate of your soul. Don't let the "doubters" in. Arrest the lies, destroy the speculations, and make your mind a "holy city" where Christ is the only authority.

Closing Prayer

Lord, I thank You that You have given me a sound mind and the power of Your Spirit. I confess that I often let my thoughts run wild and build strongholds of anxiety and pride. Today, I take up the weapons of Your Word. I choose to arrest every rogue thought and bring it into obedience to You. Help me to guard the gates of my soul and to keep my mind fixed on Your truth. Amen.

References and Further Reading

- **John Bunyan's "The Holy War":**
  https://www.gutenberg.org/files/3945/3945-h/3945-h.htm

- **Word Study: Aichmalotizo (Take Captive):**
  https://biblehub.com/greek/163.htm

- **Spurgeon's "The Battle of the Mind":**
  https://www.spurgeon.org/resource-library/sermons/the-battle-of-the-mind/

-

Reflection

Take a few minutes to reflect and meditate on what you just read. Write down your thoughts take time to pray and praise God.

_____

_____

_____

_____

_____

_____

_____

_____

_____

_____

_____

_____

_____

_____

_____

_____

_____

_____

Day 7

Make no Provision

But put on the Lord Jesus Christ, and make no provision for the flesh in regard to its lusts.
Romans 13:14

This chapter addresses the logistics of the spiritual life. In day 6, we discussed the necessity of "capturing" rogue thoughts that have already entered the mind. Now, we move to the preventative strategy: ensuring that those thoughts never have the resources to survive in the first place. Paul provides a two-fold command that involves both an "outfitting" for the journey and a "starving" of the enemy.

Chapter 7: Starving the Enemy

Key Verse: *"But put on the Lord Jesus Christ, and make no provision for the flesh in regard to its lusts."* — **Romans 13:14 (NASB)**

The Logistics of Temptation

The word Paul uses for "provision" is *pronoia*, from which we get the word "prognosis." It literally means "forethought" or "planning." In a military context, provision refers to the supply lines—the food, ammunition, and fuel required for an army to continue its campaign.

Paul is teaching us that temptation rarely "just happens." It is usually the result of a supply line we have allowed to remain open. When we "make provision," we are essentially packing a suitcase for a trip we shouldn't be taking.

To finish well, we must not only "put on" the armor of Christ but also "cut the lines" to our old nature (*the flesh*).

A Lesson from History: The Conversion of Augustine

One of the most famous moments in church history centers on this exact verse.

In the late 4th century, a brilliant but troubled man named Augustine of Hippo sat in a garden in Milan. He was torn between his intellectual belief in God and his physical addiction to a life of lust and ambition. He famously prayed, "Lord, make me pure—but not yet."

He then heard the voice of a child in a nearby house chanting, "*Tolle lege, tolle lege*" (Take up and read). Augustine picked up a scroll of Paul's letters and his eyes fell upon Romans 13:13-14.

"Not in carousing and drunkenness, not in sexual promiscuity and sensuality, not in strife and jealousy. But put on the Lord Jesus Christ, and make no provision for the flesh..."

Augustine later wrote that "a light of certainty was flooded into my heart, and all the shadows of doubt faded away." He realized he couldn't just "try harder" to be good; he had to stop making *plans* for his sin.

He finished well—becoming one of the most influential theologians in history—because he stopped packing for the "old life" and began "putting on" the new.

The "Put On" and the "Put Off"

Spiritual growth is never just about stopping a bad habit; it is about replacing it with a person.

- **"Put on the Lord Jesus Christ"**: This is the active "outfitting." It involves saturating your mind with His Word, mimicking His character, and relying on His strength.

- **"Make no provision":** This is the passive "starvation." If you struggle with greed, don't browse luxury catalogs. If you struggle with gossip, don't sit at the "lunch table of secrets." If you struggle with anger, don't "rehears" the argument in your head.

If you stop feeding a fire, it eventually goes out. If you stop feeding the flesh, its power over you begins to wither.

The 3:00 AM Decision

Finishing well requires realizing that the battle is won or lost long before the temptation arrives. The "provision" is made at 10:00 AM for the temptation that strikes at 10:00 PM.

As noted in the **P.R.E.M.I.S.E.** framework (specifically the "Mentally Positive" and "Spiritually Grounded" pillars), our choices define our trajectory. Making "no provision" means deciding *now* that you will not place yourself in a position where your "flesh" can demand a seat at the table.

Wisdom from the "Prince of Preachers"

Charles Spurgeon was a master of the "preventative" spiritual life. He understood that the heart is a "fountain," and we must guard what goes into it.

He once cautioned:

"He who carries gunpowder about him had need beware of sparks. If you know your nature to be volatile and easily set on fire, do not go into the midst of the blaze."

Spurgeon emphasized that "putting on Christ" is like wearing a garment of light that makes the "dark deeds" of the flesh look repulsive. He taught that we should be so occupied with "provisioning" ourselves with the grace of God that we have no room in our "wagon" for the baggage of the world.

How to "Make No Provision" Today

This is a discipline of "intentionality", which is the heartbeat of this book.

1. **The Proactive Audit:** Look at your recurring struggles. What are the "supply lines"? (Example: Is it a certain social media app? A

specific route you drive? A certain time of night?). Cut the line today.

2. **The "Outfitting" Prayer:** Every morning, physically mimic the "putting on" of Christ. Say, "Lord, today I put on Your patience, Your purity, and Your perspective."

3. **The H.A.L.T.** Check: As discussed in previous lessons, never make a provision for a choice when you are **Hungry, Angry, Lonely,** or **Tired.** These are the moments when the flesh most loudly demands "provisions."

By making no provision for the flesh, you stop weaving the threads of bad habits and start weaving a cable of Christ-like character.

A Moment for Reflection

Are you trying to "put on Christ" while still carrying a suitcase full of provisions for your old life? You cannot walk toward the "finish line" while holding onto the "starting line."

"Making no provision" isn't about being perfect; it's about being honest. It's about looking at your "supply lines" and having the courage to cut them. Today, don't just "capture" the thought (Chapter 30); remove the food that keeps the thought alive.

Closing Prayer

Lord, I thank You that You have provided everything I need for life and godliness. I confess that I often leave the door open for my old nature, making plans for my own failures. Today, I choose to "put on" the Lord Jesus Christ. Give me the strength to cut the supply lines to my flesh. Let my only provision be Your grace and Your Word. Amen.

References and Further Reading

- **The Confessions of Saint Augustine:**
  https://www.gutenberg.org/files/3296/3296-h/3296-h.htm

- **Word Study: Pronoia (Provision):**
  https://biblehub.com/greek/4307.htm

- **Spurgeon on "Putting on Christ":**
  https://www.spurgeon.org/resource-library/sermons/putting-on-the-lord-jesus-christ/

Reflection

Take a few minutes to reflect and meditate on what you just read. Write down your thoughts take time to pray and praise God.

_____

_____

_____

_____

_____

_____

_____

_____

_____

_____

_____

_____

_____

_____

_____

_____

_____

Day 8

Seek Justice

He has told you, O man, what is good;
And what does the Lord require of you
But to do justice, to love mercy,
And to walk humbly with your God?
Micah 6:8

For this chapter, we are diving into one of the most famous—yet most challenging—blueprints for the Christian life. Let's look at what it truly means to seek justice as a reflection of God's heart.

Chapter 8: The Three-Step Walk

Key Verse: *"He has told you, O man, what is good; and what does the Lord require of you but to do justice, to love kindness, and to walk humbly with your God?"* — **Micah 6:8 (NASB)**

The Simple, Hard Truth

Have you ever felt like the Christian life was just too complicated? Sometimes it feels like there are a thousand different rules to follow, dozens of theological books to read, and endless debates about how to live "the right way."

In the days of the prophet Micah, the people of Israel felt the same way. They were trying to please God with big, flashy sacrifices. They thought that if they just brought enough burnt offerings or poured out enough expensive oil, God would be happy. But they were missing the point entirely.

God didn't want their stuff. He wanted their hearts, and he wanted their hands to be busy doing His work. So, He gave them a simple, three-part checklist that we still use today: **Do justice. Love kindness. Walk humbly.**

Today, we're going to focus on that first command: **Doing justice.**

What is Justice, Anyway?

When we hear the word "justice," we usually think of a courtroom, a judge's gavel, or someone getting punished for a crime. But in the Bible, justice (the Hebrew word *mishpat*) is about much more than just punishment. It's about making things right. It's about looking at a broken world and saying, "That's not how God intended it to be," and then doing something to fix it.

Think about a seesaw on a playground. If a giant is sitting on one side and a toddler is on the other, the toddler is stuck high in the air, unable to move. Justice is the act of stepping in to balance that seesaw so everyone can play.

Biblical justice is proactive. It means standing up for the person who doesn't have a voice. It means being honest in our business dealings. It means caring for the "quartet of the vulnerable" that the Bible mentions over and over again: the widow, the orphan, the immigrant, and the poor.

A Lesson from History: William Wilberforce

To understand what "doing justice" looks like in the real world, we can look at a man named William Wilberforce. He lived in England in the late 1700s. At that time, the British Empire was making a lot of money from the slave trade. It was considered "just the way things were."

But Wilberforce became a Christian, and he realized he couldn't just sit in a church pew on Sundays and ignore the horror of slavery on Mondays. He realized that if he was going to follow Micah 6:8, he had to *do* justice.

He spent decades fighting in the British Parliament. He was mocked, he was threatened, and his health failed. He lost many votes before he ever won one. But he didn't give up because he knew that justice wasn't a suggestion — it was a command from God. Shortly before he died, he finally saw the slave trade abolished in the British Empire.

Wilberforce once said:

"Is it not the great end of religion, and, in particular, the glory of Christianity, to extinguish the spirit of selfishness, and to touch the heart with a tender love for our fellow-creatures?"

He understood that seeking justice is how we show the world what God's love looks like in action.

The Story of the Unfair Vineyard

Jesus told a story that helps us understand God's version of justice, which often looks different than ours. In **Matthew 20:1–16**, Jesus tells the Parable of the Vineyard Laborers.

The owner of a vineyard hires people at 6:00 AM, 9:00 AM, noon, 3:00 PM, and even 5:00 PM. At the end of the day, he pays them all the *exact same amount*. The guys who worked all day in the sun were furious! They thought it was "unfair."

But the owner reminded them that he paid them exactly what he promised. He wasn't being "unjust" to the early workers; he was being "generous" to the late ones. You see, in God's kingdom, justice is tied to his grace. Doing justice means ensuring that everyone has what they need to survive and thrive, regardless of their status or how the world views their "worth."

Justice Starts Small

You might be thinking, "I'm not a member of Parliament like Wilberforce, and I don't own a vineyard. How do I 'do justice' in my neighborhood?"

Justice usually starts with our eyes. We have to stop looking past people.

- It's noticing the coworker who is being bullied and sitting with them at lunch.

- It's choosing to buy products from companies that treat their workers fairly.

- It's speaking up when you hear someone tell a joke that demeans another person's race or background.

President Abraham Lincoln, a man who wrestled deeply with justice during the darkest time in American history, once said:

"I am not bound to win, but I am bound to be true. I am not bound to succeed, but I am bound to live up to what light I have."

God isn't asking you to fix the whole world by yourself this afternoon. He is asking you to live up to the "light" you have. He is asking you to do what is right in the square inch of the world where He has placed you.

Why Do We Do It?

We don't seek justice to "earn" our way into heaven. We can't do that. We seek justice because we serve a Just God.

In **Psalm 89:14 (NASB)**, the Bible says: "*Righteousness and justice are the foundation of Your throne; Lovingkindness and truth go before You.*"

If justice is the foundation of God's throne, then it should be the foundation of our lives. When we fight for what is right, we are acting like our Heavenly Father. We are showing a skeptical world that God cares about their pain, their hunger, and their dignity.

A Moment for Reflection

Take a minute to think about your community. Who are the people who are being "pushed down" on the seesaw? Maybe it's a neighbor going through a messy divorce, a kid at school who doesn't have the right clothes, or a local family struggling to pay for groceries.

Doing justice isn't a feeling; it's a verb. It requires movement. It might be uncomfortable. It might cost you time or money. But when we do it, we find ourselves walking right next to God.

As the great theologian St. Augustine of Hippo said:

"Charity is no substitute for justice withheld."

We can't just give people "handouts" and think we've fulfilled Micah 6:8. We have to look at the systems that make people poor or keep them oppressed and ask, "How can I help make this right?"

Closing Prayer

Lord, thank You for being a God of perfect justice and perfect mercy. Open my eyes today to see the people I usually ignore. Give me the courage to speak up when I see something wrong, and the strength to do what is right even when it's hard. Help me to not just talk about justice, but to do it. Amen.

References and Further Reading

- **The Life of William Wilberforce:**
  https://www.christianitytoday.com/history/people/activists/william-wilberforce.html

- **Abraham Lincoln's Quotes on Truth and Duty:**
  https://www.nps.gov/libo/learn/historyculture/lincoln-quotes.htm

- **Understanding "Mishpat" (Biblical Justice):**
  https://bibleproject.com/explore/video/justice/

-

Reflection

Take a few minutes to reflect and meditate on what you just read.   Write down your thoughts take time to pray and praise God.

_____

_____

_____

_____

_____

_____

_____

_____

_____

_____

_____

_____

_____

_____

_____

_____

_____

Day 9

Love Mercy

He has told you, O man, what is good;
And what does the Lord require of you
But to do justice, to love mercy,
And to walk humbly with your God?
Micah 6:8

It is a joy to continue this journey with you. While "doing justice" focuses on our hands and our actions in the world, "loving mercy" focuses on the posture of our hearts. It's often the bridge between doing what is right and walking with God.

Chapter 9: The Heart That Delights in Mercy

Key Verse: *"He has told you, O man, what is good; and what does the Lord require of you but to do justice, to love kindness, and to walk humbly with your God?"* — **Micah 6:8 (NASB)**

*(Note: Many scholars note that the word "kindness" in the NASB translation of this verse comes from the Hebrew word **hesed**, which is frequently translated as "mercy" or "steadfast love.")*

More Than Just "Being Nice"

In our last chapter, we talked about "doing justice"—standing up for what is right and fixing what is broken. But if we do justice without mercy, we can easily become cold, self-righteous, or even mean. That's why the second requirement in Micah 6:8 is to **love mercy.**

Notice that God doesn't just say "do" mercy. He says we should *love* it.

Think about something you truly love. Maybe it's a hobby, a favorite meal, or a person. When you love something, you seek it out. You delight in it. You want more of it. God is asking us to have that same kind of passion for showing mercy to others.

What is Mercy?

In the simplest terms, mercy is not giving someone the punishment they actually deserve. If justice is getting what you deserve, mercy is *not* getting the "bad" you deserve.

But biblical mercy — that word *hesed* — is even deeper. It's a loyal, sacrificial kind of love. It's the way a parent looks at a child who has made a mess. The parent might be frustrated, but their love for the child is so strong that they move toward them to help clean it up rather than just standing back to scold them.

A Lesson from History: C.S. Lewis and the Grudge

The famous author and theologian C.S. Lewis once wrote deeply about the struggle to be merciful and forgiving. Before he became a Christian, he was a man who held onto logic and "fairness." But after his conversion, he realized that mercy was the very oxygen of the Christian life.

Lewis once remarked:

"To be a Christian means to forgive the inexcusable because God has forgiven the inexcusable in you."

Lewis understood that mercy isn't something we do because the other person earned it. If they earned it, it wouldn't be mercy! We do it because we remember how much mercy we have received from God.

The Story of the Unmerciful Servant

Jesus told a powerful (and a bit convicting) story about this in **Matthew 18:21–35 (NASB)**.

A king decided to settle accounts with his servants. One man owed him a massive amount of money — thousands of lifetimes' worth of wages. The man couldn't pay, so the king ordered him and his family to be sold into slavery. The servant fell on his knees and begged for patience.

Then, something incredible happened. The king didn't just give him more time; he canceled the entire debt! That is extreme mercy.

But then, that same servant went out and found a fellow servant who owed him a tiny amount of money — maybe a few months' wages. He grabbed him by the throat and demanded payment. When the second servant begged for mercy, the first servant refused and threw him in prison.

When the king found out, he was furious. He called the first servant "wicked" because he had received a mountain of mercy but refused to give even a tiny molehill of mercy to someone else.

The lesson for us is clear: We love mercy because we have been drowned in it. When we refuse to show mercy to a spouse, a neighbor, or a coworker, we are acting like that ungrateful servant.

Mercy in the Small Things

Loving mercy changes how we react to the daily annoyances of life.

- **On the Road:** When someone cuts you off in traffic, justice says they deserve a honk and a dirty look. Mercy says, "Maybe they are having a terrible day or rushing to the hospital," and lets it go.

- **At Home:** When a family member forgets a chore for the tenth time, justice says they deserve a lecture. Mercy looks for a way to help them remember without shaming them.

- **In the Church:** When a fellow believer falls into sin or makes a mistake, mercy doesn't gossip about it. Mercy prays for them and looks for a way to help them get back on their feet.

The great American statesman Daniel Webster once said:

"Justice, sir, is the great interest of man on earth. It is the ligament which holds civilized beings and civilized nations together."

While Webster was right about justice, we could add that **mercy** is the oil that keeps those ligaments from grinding together and causing pain. Justice holds us together, but mercy makes the "holding" beautiful.

Why Do We Struggle to Love Mercy?

Most of us struggle with mercy because we like being "right." We like the feeling of having the moral high ground. We want the person who hurt us to feel the weight of what they did.

But the Bible tells us in **James 2:13 (NASB)**: *"For judgment will be merciless to one who has shown no mercy; mercy triumphs over judgment."*

When we choose mercy, we aren't saying that the wrong thing was "okay." We are saying that our relationship with that person, and our desire to be like Jesus, is more important than our right to be angry.

The Example of Robert E. Lee

Regardless of the complex history surrounding the Civil War, there is a famous anecdote about General Robert E. Lee after the war ended. A woman showed him a tree in her yard that had been severely damaged by Union artillery fire. She looked for him to condemn the North and join her in her bitterness.

Instead, Lee looked at her and said:

"Cut it down, my dear madam, and forget it."

He knew that holding onto the evidence of past hurts only keeps the heart in a cage. Loving mercy means having the courage to "cut down" the trees of bitterness in our own lives.

A Moment for Reflection

Is there someone in your life right now who "deserves" your anger? Someone who messed up, let you down, or treated you unfairly?

Now, think about your own life. Think about the mistakes you've made — the ones nobody knows about. Think about how God has responded to you. He didn't come at you with a gavel; He came to you with a Cross.

If you want to "love mercy" today, start by thanking God for the mercy He showed you this morning. Then, ask Him for the strength to pass a little bit of that mercy along to someone else.

Closing Prayer

Heavenly Father, thank You for Your steadfast love (hesed) that never ceases. I confess that I often prefer justice for others and mercy for myself. Change my heart so that I truly love mercy. Help me to be quick to forgive and slow to judge. Let my life be a reflection of the grace You have poured out on me through Jesus Christ. Amen.

References and Further Reading

- **C.S. Lewis on Forgiveness:** https://www.cslewis.com/the-weight-of-glory-and-the-practice-of-forgiveness/

- **The Meaning of "Hesed":** https://bibleproject.com/explore/video/loyal-love/

- **Robert E. Lee and the Damaged Tree:** https://www.battlefields.org/learn/articles/robert-e-lee-biography

- **Daniel Webster's Remarks on Justice:** https://www.dartmouth.edu/~dwebster/quotes.html

Reflection

Take a few minutes to reflect and meditate on what you just read. Write down your thoughts take time to pray and praise God.

_____

_____

_____

_____

_____

_____

_____

_____

_____

_____

_____

_____

_____

_____

_____

_____

_____

_____

_____

Day 10

Walk Humbly

He has told you, O man, what is good;
And what does the Lord require of you
But to do justice, to love mercy,
And to walk humbly with your God?
Micah 6:8

It's a privilege to wrap up this "Micah 6:8 Trilogy" with you. We've looked at our hands (Doing Justice) and our hearts (Loving Mercy). Now, we look at our feet and our direction: **Walking Humbly.** This is where the Christian life moves from a list of duties to a living, breathing relationship.

Chapter 10: The Lowly Path to Greatness

Key Verse: *"He has told you, O man, what is good; and what does the Lord require of you but to do justice, to love kindness, and to walk humbly with your God?"* — **Micah 6:8 (NASB)**

The Third Requirement

Imagine you are invited to go for a hike with the most famous, brilliant, and powerful person in the world. How would you act? You probably wouldn't try to push them out of the way to lead the group. You wouldn't spend the whole time bragging about your own small achievements. You would likely walk a little behind them, listening carefully to every word they said, just happy to be in their presence.

This is the picture Micah gives us for the Christian life. After we have learned to do justice and love mercy, God gives us the final piece of the puzzle: **Walk humbly with your God.**

It is interesting that God doesn't say "run for your God" or "work for your God." He says *walk with* Him. Walking is a steady, daily activity. It implies a long-term relationship. But there's a catch—you can't walk with God if you are trying to be the center of attention. You have to be humble.

What Does It Mean to Walk Humbly?

Humility is one of those words we often misunderstand. We sometimes think it means thinking poorly of ourselves or walking around with our heads down, acting like we aren't good at anything.

But true biblical humility isn't about thinking *less* of yourself; it's about thinking of yourself *less*. It's realizing that you aren't the main character of the universe—God is. When we walk humbly, we recognize that every breath we take, every talent we have, and every success we achieve is a gift from Him.

As the great British Prime Minister Winston Churchill once said about a political rival:

"He is a modest man, who has much to be modest about."

While Churchill was being a bit cheeky, the truth is that when we stand next to a holy, infinite God, we *all* have "much to be modest about." Humility is simply being honest about who we are in relation to who God is.

A Lesson from History: Booker T. Washington

One of the greatest examples of walking humbly in American history is Booker T. Washington. He was born into slavery but rose to become one of the most influential educators and advisors to presidents.

There is a famous story about him when he was the president of the Tuskegee Institute. He was walking through a wealthy neighborhood when a woman, not recognizing him, called out to him. She asked if he would like to earn a few dollars by chopping wood for her.

Now, a proud man would have been offended. He could have said, "Do you know who I am? I am a college president!" But Washington simply smiled, took off his coat, and chopped the wood. He carried it into her house and then went on his way.

Later, a neighbor told the woman who the man really was. Embarrassed, she went to his office the next day to apologize. Washington replied, "It's quite all right, madam. I like to help my friends whenever I can."

Washington lived out the truth that no task is too small for a person who is walking humbly with God. He wasn't worried about his "status" because his identity was rooted in something much deeper than human praise.

The Story of the Pharisee and the Tax Collector

Jesus gave us a vivid contrast of what humility looks like in **Luke 18:9–14 (NASB)**. He told a story about two men who went to the Temple to pray.

One was a Pharisee—a religious leader who followed every rule. He stood up and prayed about how great he was! He thanked God that he wasn't like "other people" and listed all his good deeds. He was "walking," but he was walking alone, fueled by his own pride.

The other man was a tax collector, someone generally hated by society. He wouldn't even look up to heaven. He beat his chest and said, *"God, be merciful to me, the sinner!"*

Jesus said that it was the tax collector—the humble man—who went home justified before God. Why? Because you cannot walk *with* God if you are full of yourself. Pride creates a wall; humility creates a path.

The Benefit of the "Lowly" Walk

Why does God require us to walk humbly? Is it because He wants to squash our confidence? Not at all! It's because humility is the only place where we can truly find peace.

When you are proud, you are always worried about what people think of you. You are always exhausted from trying to prove you are the best. But when you walk humbly, that weight is lifted. You don't have to be the best; you just have to be *His*.

In **1 Peter 5:5 (NASB)**, the Bible tells us: *"God is opposed to the proud, but gives grace to the humble."* Think about that. If we are proud, we are actually putting ourselves in opposition to God. We are trying to fight the One who created the stars! But when we humble ourselves, God opens the floodgates of His grace.

How to Practice the Humble Walk

How do we actually do this on a Tuesday morning?

1. **Listen More Than You Speak:** A humble person knows they don't have all the answers. They are willing to learn from God's Word and from other people.

2. **Admit When You Are Wrong:** Nothing kills pride faster than the words, "I'm sorry, I was wrong. Will you forgive me?"

3. **Give Away the Credit:** When something goes well at work or at home, point to God and point to the others who helped you.

The great Christian apologist and author G.K. Chesterton once wrote:

"Humility is the mother of giants. One sees great things from the valley; only small things from the peak."

When we think we are at the "peak" of our own importance, everything else looks small. But when we walk in the "valley" of humility, we see how truly great and massive God's love and power really are.

A Moment for Reflection

Are you trying to lead God today, or are you following Him?

Pride says, "God, here is my plan, please bless it." Humility says, "God, here is my life, please lead it."

Walking humbly means trusting that God knows the way better than you do. It means being okay with not being noticed, as long as He is honored.

Today, as you go about your business, try to "lower your volume." Let God be the big voice in your life, and see how much more peaceful the walk becomes.

Closing Prayer

Lord, I admit that I like to be in charge. I like to be right, and I like to be noticed. Please forgive my pride. Help me to take my place beside You, not in front of You. Teach me to walk at Your pace and to find my joy in Your presence rather than in the praise of others. Thank You for the grace You give to the humble. Amen.

References and Further Reading

- **Biography of Booker T. Washington:**
  https://www.biography.com/activist/booker-t-washington

- **Winston Churchill's Famous Wit:**
  https://www.winstonchurchill.org/resources/quotes/

- **G.K. Chesterton on the Virtue of Humility:**
  https://www.chesterton.org/humility/

- **The Pharisee and the Tax Collector Commentary:**
  https://www.biblegateway.com/resources/commentary/IVP-NT/Luke/Parable-Pharisee-Tax-Collector

Reflection

Take a few minutes to reflect and meditate on what you just read. Write down your thoughts take time to pray and praise God.

_____

_____

_____

_____

_____

_____

_____

_____

_____

_____

_____

_____

_____

_____

_____

_____

_____

Day 11

Dwell

Finally, brethren, whatever is true, whatever is honorable, whatever is right, whatever is pure, whatever is lovely, whatever is of good repute, if there is any excellence and if anything worthy of praise, dwell on these things.
Philippians 4:8

We've spent the last three chapters looking at our outward actions and our humble posture before God. Now, we are moving into the "command center" of the Christian life: **the mind.** In a world that is constantly screaming for our attention with bad news, social media drama, and personal worries, Philippians 4:8 acts like a filter for our souls.

Chapter 11: The Gatekeeper of Your Mind

Key Verse: *"Finally, brethren, whatever is true, whatever is honorable, whatever is right, whatever is pure, whatever is lovely, whatever is of good repute, if there is any excellence and if anything worthy of praise, dwell on these things."* —
Philippians 4:8 (NASB)

The Battle for Your Thoughts

Have you ever noticed that your mood usually follows your thoughts? If you spend your whole morning thinking about everything that could go wrong at work, you'll probably arrive at the office feeling anxious and defeated. If you spend your evening scrolling through negative news stories, you'll likely go to bed feeling hopeless.

Our minds are like a garden. If we don't intentionally plant flowers, weeds will grow all by themselves. We don't have to "try" to have negative thoughts; they just seem to show up. But the Apostle Paul gives us a command that changes everything: We are told to **dwell** on specific things.

The word "dwell" in this verse (the Greek word *logizomai*) means more than just a passing thought. It's a mathematical term! It means to "calculate," "reckon," or "take into account." It's an active choice to let certain ideas take up permanent residence in our brains.

The Power of What We Dwell Upon

What we think about determines who we become. This isn't just "positive thinking" or a self-help trick; it's a spiritual reality.

Think about a sponge. If you soak a sponge in vinegar, you can't be surprised when you squeeze it and vinegar comes out. If we soak our minds in fear, anger, or worldly gossip, those are the things that will come out when life "squeezes" us with stress or hardship.

A Lesson from History: Admiral James Stockdale

One of the most powerful examples of "dwelling" on the right things comes from Admiral James Stockdale, one of the highest-ranking naval officers to be held as a prisoner of war in Vietnam. He was tortured and held in isolation for over seven years.

How did he survive? He practiced what is now called the "Stockdale Paradox." He never lost faith that he would eventually get out, but he also faced the brutal facts of his current reality.

Most importantly, he chose what to dwell on. Instead of dwelling on his pain or the cruelty of his captors, he focused on his duty, his integrity, and the "true" and "honorable" values of his country and his faith.

He didn't let the prison walls get inside his head. He realized that while his captors could control his body, they couldn't control what he chose to "calculate" or dwell upon in his mind.

The Eightfold Filter

Paul gives us a checklist of eight things that should be allowed past the "gatekeeper" of our minds. Let's look at a few of them:

- **Whatever is True:** In a world of "fake news" and lies, we must dwell on the truth of God's Word.

- **Whatever is Honorable:** This refers to things that are noble and worthy of respect, not things that are cheap or degrading.

- **Whatever is Lovely:** This is about beauty! God created the world with beauty, and we should notice it.

- **Whatever is Worthy of Praise:** If it's not something you'd be happy to praise God for, it probably shouldn't be the main thing you're thinking about.

If a thought doesn't pass these tests, Paul says we shouldn't let it stay. We might see a negative thought fly by, but we don't have to invite it in for dinner!

The Story of the Two Wolves

There is a famous old anecdote (often attributed to various cultures) about a grandfather talking to his grandson. He says, "There are two wolves fighting inside of me. One is full of anger, envy, and greed. The other is full of joy, peace, and truth."

The grandson asks, "Which one wins?"

The grandfather replies, "The one I feed."

When we obey Philippians 4:8, we are choosing which "wolf" to feed. When we dwell on God's promises, we are feeding our faith. When we dwell on our problems, we are feeding our fears.

Advice from the "Prince of Preachers"

Charles Spurgeon, the famous 19th-century preacher, knew a lot about the battle of the mind. He often struggled with deep bouts of depression. Yet, he constantly urged his congregation to dwell on the character of God.

Spurgeon once said:

"The mind can descend far lower than the body, for in it there are bottomless pits. The flesh can bear only a certain number of wounds and no more, but the soul can be bled in ten thousand ways, and die every day."

Because he knew how dark the mind could get, he was even more adamant that we must anchor our thoughts to what is "true" and "excellent." He knew that we cannot think our way out of a dark hole, but we can *dwell* our way into the light of God's presence.

Practical Steps to "Dwell" Correctly

How do we actually do this? It's not about ignoring reality; it's about choosing our focus.

1. **The Morning Pivot:** Before you check your phone or the news, read one verse of Scripture. Let that "True" thing be the first thing your mind calculates for the day.

2. **The "Check Your Intake" Test:** Ask yourself, "Is this movie/book/conversation making me feel more like Jesus or more like the world?" If it's not "honorable" or "pure," turn it off.

3. **Gratitude Journals:** Writing down three "praiseworthy" things every night forces your brain to look for the "lovely" during the day.

The great scientist Isaac Newton, a man who used his mind to discover the laws of gravity and motion, was also a deeply religious man. He said:

"I can take my telescope and look millions of miles into space; but I can lay it aside and go into my room and in prayer get nearer to God and heaven than I can assist by all the assistance of telescopes and helioscopes."

Newton knew that as brilliant as his scientific thoughts were, dwelling on the Creator was the highest use of his mind.

A Moment for Reflection

Take a mental "inventory" of your last hour. What have you been dwelling on? Has it been the "right" and "pure" things of God, or has it been a mental replay of an argument you had? Has it been the "excellence" of God's creation, or the "bad repute" of a neighbor?

You have more power over your thoughts than you think. You are the gatekeeper. Today, when a thought knocks on the door of your mind, ask it for its credentials. If it isn't true, honorable, or lovely, don't let it in.

Closing Prayer

Lord, I thank You for the gift of my mind. I confess that I often let it wander into dark and anxious places. Please help me to be a better gatekeeper today. Teach me to dwell on Your truth, to notice Your beauty, and to celebrate what is excellent in others. May the thoughts of my heart be pleasing to You. Amen.

References and Further Reading

- **The Stockdale Paradox and Mental Resilience:**
  https://www.jimcollins.com/concepts/the-stockdale-paradox.html

- **Charles Spurgeon on Depression and Faith:**
  https://www.spurgeon.org/resource-library/blog-posts/the-pastors-fainting-fits/

- **Isaac Newton's Faith and Science:**
  https://www.bbvaopenmind.com/en/science/leading-figures/isaac-newton-the-scientist-who-studied-the-bible/

- **Understanding "Logizomai" (Dwell):**
  https://www.blueletterbible.org/lexicon/g3049/nasb95/mgnt/0-1/

Reflection

Take a few minutes to reflect and meditate on what you just read. Write down your thoughts take time to pray and praise God.

_____

_____

_____

_____

_____

_____

_____

_____

_____

_____

_____

_____

_____

_____

_____

_____

_____

Day 12

Set Your Mind

Set your mind on the things above, not on the things that are on earth.
Colossians 3:2

This is the perfect companion to our study of Philippians 4:8. While the last chapter taught us *what* to think about (the quality of our thoughts), this chapter focuses on the *direction* of our thoughts. It's about the "setting" on the compass of our souls.

Chapter 12: Setting the Spiritual Compass

Key Verse: *"Set your mind on the things above, not on the things that are on earth."* — **Colossians 3:2 (NASB)**

The Internal GPS

Have you ever used a GPS to get somewhere? Before you start driving, you have to "set" the destination. Once the destination is locked in, the GPS doesn't care about the gas stations you pass, the billboards on the side of the road, or the stray dog running across a field. It stays focused on where you are going.

The Apostle Paul tells us that our minds have a similar setting. We are commanded to **set our minds on things above.** The Greek word used for "set your mind" is *phroneite*. It's a word that describes an intentional, persistent inner pull. It's not just a passing thought about heaven while you're singing a hymn; it's an active decision to let the reality of God's kingdom be the "North Star" for your life.

The Problem with "Earthly" Vision

Paul warns us not to set our minds on "the things that are on earth." Now, Paul isn't saying we should ignore our jobs, our families, or our taxes. We live on earth, and we have responsibilities here.

However, "setting your mind on earthly things" means letting the temporary stuff of this world — money, status, physical comfort, or the opinions of others — be the boss of your emotions.

Think of it like being on a cruise ship. If you set your mind only on the "earthly" things of the ship — the buffet, the pool, the decor — you might forget that the ship is actually taking you to a destination. If the buffet runs out of shrimp, your whole world falls apart. But if your mind is set on the destination (the "things above"), you can handle a little trouble on the ship because you know you're almost home.

A Lesson from History: Florence Nightingale

Florence Nightingale is famous for being the founder of modern nursing, but many people don't realize she was a woman deeply driven by a "mind set on things above."

In the 1850s, during the Crimean War, she went into horrific hospital conditions where soldiers were dying more from filth and disease than from bullets. The "earthly" perspective told her it was a lost cause, that it was too dirty for a lady of her social standing, and that she should just go back to her comfortable life in England.

But Nightingale believed she had a "divine calling." She set her mind on God's requirement for compassion and healing. Because her mind was set on "things above," she had the strength to endure the "things on earth" — the stench, the lack of supplies, and the pushback from military doctors.

She once wrote:

"God's kingdom is within us. But we must also create it without, by making it visible in our lives."

By focusing on the eternal value of a human soul, she changed the world of medicine forever.

The Vertical Life

Living with a mind "set on things above" changes the way we see our daily problems.

Imagine you are looking at a giant mountain from an inch away. All you see is a gray, rough wall. It's overwhelming! But if you step back and look at it from a thousand feet up, you see the beauty of the peak, the forest below, and the path leading home.

When we set our mind on "things above," we are looking at our lives from God's perspective.

- **In Traffic:** Instead of just seeing a red light, we see an opportunity to pray for the people in the cars around us.

- **In Financial Stress:** Instead of just seeing a bank balance, we see a God who promises to provide for His children.

- **In Grief:** Instead of just seeing a grave, we see the promise of the Resurrection.

The Story of the Two Travelers

There is an old story about two men traveling to a distant city. One man spent his whole journey complaining about the dust on his boots, the hardness of his bed at the inn, and the bad weather. He arrived at the city tired, grumpy, and miserable.

The second man walked the same road, faced the same dust, and slept in the same hard beds. But he spent the whole time talking about the king he was going to see and the beautiful home that was waiting for him. He arrived at the city with a smile on his face.

The difference wasn't the "earthly" road; it was where they had "set" their minds.

Wisdom from a Founding Father

Benjamin Franklin was a man of immense earthly achievement—he was an inventor, a writer, and a diplomat. Yet, he understood that the things of this world were not the end of the story.

Franklin famously wrote his own epitaph when he was a young man, comparing his body to an old book. He wrote:

"The Body of B. Franklin, Printer... Like the Cover of an old Book, Its Contents torn out, And stript of its Lettering and Gilding, Lies here, Food for Worms. But the Work shall not be lost; For it will, as he believ'd, appear once more, In a new and more elegant Edition, Corrected and improved by the Author."

Even a man as busy with "earthly" things as Franklin understood that the "Author" (God) had an eternal plan that was far more important than the "Gilding" (wealth and fame) of this life.

How to "Reset" Your Mind

It's easy for our minds to drift back down to earth. Gravity works on our souls just like it works on our bodies! Here are three ways to "reset" your spiritual GPS:

1. **The "Heavenly" Filter:** When you are worried, ask yourself: "Will this matter 100 years from now?" If the answer is no, it's an earthly thing. Don't let it sit in the captain's chair of your mind.

2. **Read the Destination Map:** You can't set your mind on things above if you don't know what they are. Spend time in the Gospels. See how Jesus treated people. See what He valued.

3. **Practice Vertical Conversation:** Throughout the day, send up "arrow prayers" — short, one-sentence prayers like, "Lord, help me see this person the way You see them." This keeps the connection to "above" open.

As the great reformer Martin Luther once said:

"I have held many things in my hands, and I have lost them all; but whatever I have placed in God's hands, that I still possess."

When we set our minds on things above, we are placing our treasure where it can never be lost.

A Moment for Reflection

What is the "default setting" of your mind today? If you aren't intentionally thinking about anything, where does your mind go? Does it go to your worries? Your bank account? Your "to-do" list?

Today, try a "manual override." When you feel your mind sinking into the "earthly" mud of stress or jealousy, pause and look up. Remind yourself that you are a citizen of heaven, a child of the King, and that your journey on this earth is just a short walk to a beautiful home.

Closing Prayer

Lord, I admit that my eyes are often glued to the ground. I get so worried about earthly things that I forget I am Yours. Please help me to "reset" my mind today. Give me a heavenly perspective on my problems and an eternal hope in my heart. Teach me to walk on earth while keeping my heart in heaven. Amen.

References and Further Reading

- **The Spiritual Life of Florence Nightingale:**
  https://www.florence-nightingale.co.uk/healthcare-and-religion/

- **Benjamin Franklin's Epitaph and Beliefs:**
  https://www.fi.edu/en/science-and-education/benjamin-franklin/epitaph

- **Martin Luther on Trusting God:**
  https://www.lutheranworld.org/content/martin-luther-quotes

- **Word Study: Phroneite (Set Your Mind):**
  https://biblehub.com/greek/5426.htm

Reflection

Take a few minutes to reflect and meditate on what you just read. Write down your thoughts take time to pray and praise God.

_____

_____

_____

_____

_____

_____

_____

_____

_____

_____

_____

_____

Day 13

Draw Near

Draw near to God and He will draw near to you. Cleanse your hands, you sinners; and purify your hearts, you double-minded.

James 4:8

This is a beautiful and intimate command to explore. We've talked about the "gatekeeping" of our thoughts and "setting" our mental GPS toward heaven. Now, we look at the actual movement of our souls. This chapter is about the invitation to bridge the gap between us and our Creator.

Chapter 13: The Promise of the Open Door

Key Verse: *"Draw near to God and He will draw near to you."* — **James 4:8 (NASB)**

A Two-Way Street

Have you ever wanted to be friends with someone but felt like they were too important or too busy for you? Maybe it was a boss at work, a local leader, or even a distant relative. You might have waited for them to notice you first, fearing that if you reached out, you'd be ignored.

When it comes to God, many people feel the same way. We think of God as a distant King on a high throne, far away from our small, messy lives. We wait for a "sign" or a bolt of lightning to feel His presence. But James 4:8 gives us an incredible promise that flips that idea upside down.

God says, "You move first, and I promise I will move too."

Drawing near to God isn't about physical distance — because God is everywhere. It's about **relational distance**. It's like two people sitting on the same couch but looking at their phones; they are physically close but miles apart. To "draw near" is to put down the phone, turn your head, and start the conversation.

The Motion of the Soul

The command to "draw near" (the Greek word *eggizo*) implies a deliberate movement. It's the same word used in ancient times for a priest approaching the altar in the Temple. It wasn't something they did by accident. It was a focused, intentional walk.

God is not hiding from you. He is not playing a game of "hide and seek." He is more like a father standing at the end of a hallway with His arms open wide. He is waiting for you to take that first step so He can rush to meet you.

A Lesson from History: Blaise Pascal

Blaise Pascal was one of the greatest mathematicians and physicists in history. You might recognize his name from your science textbooks (like Pascal's Law). But Pascal was also a man who desperately wanted to "draw near" to God.

For a long time, he tried to find God only through his brain and his logic. But on the night of November 23, 1654, he had a profound spiritual experience. He felt the presence of God so strongly that he wrote about it on a piece of parchment and sewed it into the lining of his coat so he would always have it near his heart.

Pascal famously wrote:

"The heart has its reasons which reason knows nothing of... It is the heart which perceives God and not the reason. That is what faith is: God perceived by the heart, not by the reason."

Pascal realized that "drawing near" isn't a math problem to solve; it's a relationship to enjoy. He stopped just *calculating* about God and started *talking* to Him.

The Story of the Prodigal Son's Father

Jesus gave us the ultimate "picture" of James 4:8 in the story of the Prodigal Son (**Luke 15:11–32**).

You remember the story: the son runs away, spends all his father's money, and ends up feeding pigs in a far-off country. He decides to go home, hoping his father will at least hire him as a servant. He starts "drawing near" to his home, probably rehearsing a speech and feeling full of shame.

But the Bible says that while the son was "still a long way off," the father saw him. And what did the father do? He didn't sit on the porch and wait for the son to beg. He **ran** to him.

That is exactly what James 4:8 is promising. When you turn your heart toward home, God doesn't just wait for you to arrive; He runs to meet you in the middle of the road.

How Do We Draw Near?

If drawing near to God is an intentional move, what does that look like in our busy, modern lives?

- **Honesty (The Clean Hands):** If you read the rest of James 4:8, it says, "Cleanse your hands... and purify your hearts." Drawing near starts with being honest about our sins. You can't get close to someone while you're hiding a secret from them.

- **Prayer (The Conversation):** You don't need fancy words. Drawing near is as simple as saying, "Lord, I'm here. I need You today."

- **Silence (The Listening):** Sometimes we don't feel God is near because we are making too much noise. Drawing near often means turning off the radio or the TV and just sitting quietly with the Word of God.

The great American scientist George Washington Carver, who was born into slavery and became a world-renowned inventor, used to "draw near" to God every morning in a very practical way. He would go into the woods at 4:00 AM to talk to God.

Carver once said:

"I love to think of nature as an unlimited broadcasting station, through which God speaks to us every hour, if we will only tune in."

Carver knew that God was always "broadcasting," but he had to "draw near" to the radio to hear the signal.

The Result of Drawing Near

When we draw near to God, something changes in us. We start to pick up His "scent." We start to think like He thinks and love like He loves.

The famous author and preacher A.W. Tozer once said:

"To have found God and still to pursue Him is the soul's paradox of love."

The more you draw near to God, the more you realize how much more of Him there is to discover. It's not a one-time event; it's a lifelong pursuit that gets better with every step.

A Moment for Reflection

Where is your heart "located" today? Are you standing "a long way off" because you feel guilty, busy, or just plain bored?

The door is wide open. God is not waiting for you to be perfect before you approach Him. He is waiting for you to be *present*.

Today, find five minutes where you can be completely alone. No phone, no music, no distractions. Just tell God, "I am drawing near to You right now. Please draw near to me." Then, pay attention to the peace that starts to fill your heart. That peace is the sound of His footsteps coming to meet you.

Closing Prayer

Heavenly Father, I thank You that You aren't a distant God. Thank You for the promise that if I move toward You, You will move toward me. Forgive me for the times I've stayed far away, trying to do life on my own. I am drawing near to You today with all my mess and all my questions. Please meet me here. Amen.

References and Further Reading

- **Blaise Pascal's "Night of Fire":**
  https://www.christianitytoday.com/history/people/innerlife/blaise-pascal.html

- **George Washington Carver's Faith:**
  https://www.nps.gov/gwca/learn/historyculture/index.htm

- **A.W. Tozer on Pursuing God:**
  https://www.cmalliance.org/about/history/tozer/

- **Word Study: Eggizo (Draw Near):**
  https://biblehub.com/greek/1448.htm

Reflection

Take a few minutes to reflect and meditate on what you just read. Write down your thoughts take time to pray and praise God.

_____

_____

_____

_____

_____

_____

_____

_____

_____

_____

_____

_____

_____

_____

_____

Day 14

Commit Your Works

Commit your works to the Lord And your plans will be established.
Proverbs 16:3

This is a perfect follow-up to our last few chapters. We have talked about our thoughts and our relationship with God; now we are moving back into the world of action. In a culture that is obsessed with "hustle," Proverbs 16:3 gives us a completely different way to look at our daily work and our big plans.

Chapter 14: The Secret to Successful Plans

Key Verse: *"Commit your works to the Lord and your plans will be established."*
— **Proverbs 16:3 (NASB)**

The Burden of Success

Have you ever started a project—maybe a new job, a home renovation, or even a diet—and felt the crushing weight of making sure it succeeds? We often carry our "works" like a heavy backpack. We worry about every detail, we stay up late stressing over the "what-ifs," and we feel like if things fail, it's entirely on us.

King Solomon, the author of most of Proverbs, was a man who knew all about big projects. He built the Temple in Jerusalem, managed a massive kingdom, and handled incredible wealth. But he knew a secret that many high-achievers miss: True success doesn't come from gripping your work tighter. It comes from letting go.

What Does it Mean to "Commit"?

The word "commit" in the original Hebrew language (*galal*) is a very "earthy" word. It literally means **to roll.** Think about a person carrying a heavy stone that is too big to lift. Instead of trying to carry it on their back, they roll it onto a cart or roll it down a hill toward its destination.

When God tells us to commit our works to Him, He is saying, "Take that heavy project, that difficult conversation, or that big dream, and **roll it over onto Me.**" It's an act of transfer. You are moving the burden of the outcome from your shoulders to His.

A Lesson from History: George Müller

George Müller was a man who lived in Bristol, England, in the 1800s. He felt called by God to care for orphans, but he didn't have any money. In fact, he decided he would never ask a single person for a donation. Instead, he would simply "roll" his needs onto God.

Müller started with one house and 30 children. Over his lifetime, he cared for over 10,000 orphans and built massive homes for them. He received millions of dollars without ever sending out a single fundraising letter. Every morning, he committed his "works" — the food for the day, the rent, the clothes — to the Lord.

There were many times when they sat down at a breakfast table with empty bowls, and Müller would pray, thanking God for the food he knew was coming. Within minutes, a baker would knock on the door or a milkman's cart would break down right in front of the orphanage, and they would have exactly what they needed.

Müller once said:

"The beginning of anxiety is the end of faith, and the beginning of true faith is the end of anxiety."

By rolling his "works" onto God, Müller was able to live without the crushing weight of stress, even though he had thousands of children counting on him.

The Divine Partnership

It's important to notice the order of this verse. It doesn't say "make your plans and then ask God to bless them." It says commit your *works* (the things you are doing right now) and *then* your plans will be established.

When we commit our daily tasks to God, He begins to align our desires with His.

- If you are a teacher, you say, "Lord, these students are Yours. I commit my lesson plan to You today."

- If you are a parent, you say, "Lord, this child is Yours. I commit this difficult conversation to You."

- If you are a business owner, you say, "Lord, this company is Yours. I commit this deal to You."

When you do this, your "plans" are no longer just *your* plans. They become part of God's plan. And since God's plans cannot be defeated, your path becomes "established" or firm.

The Story of the Two Builders

Jesus told a story that illustrates what it looks like to have an "established" plan in **Matthew 7:24–27**.

One man built his house on the sand. He probably had great plans and worked very hard. But he didn't commit his work to a solid foundation. When the storms came, the house fell flat.

The other man built on the rock. When the same storm hit, the house stood firm. Committing your works to the Lord is like building on the rock. It doesn't mean the storms won't come—the rain falls on the righteous and the unrighteous alike—but it means that when the storm is over, your work will still be standing because it was anchored in Him.

The Wisdom of "The Great Emancipator"

President Abraham Lincoln faced the most difficult "work" imaginable: trying to keep a nation together during a bloody Civil War. He was constantly surrounded by critics and faced impossible choices.

Lincoln understood that he couldn't carry the weight of the Union on his own. He famously said:

"I have been driven many times upon my knees by the overwhelming conviction that I had nowhere else to go. My own wisdom and that of all about me seemed insufficient for that day."

Lincoln was "rolling" the weight of a nation onto the only One strong enough to carry it. He knew that if he tried to establish the plans himself, he would fail. But if he committed the work to God, the results were in better hands.

How to "Roll" Your Work Today

"Rolling" your work isn't a one-time event; it's a habit. Here is how you can practice Proverbs 16:3 today:

1. **The Morning Hand-Off:** As you look at your to-do list, literally hold it up to God and say, "Lord, I will do the work, but I give the results to You."

2. **The "Check Your Grip" Test:** If you find yourself feeling angry or panicked because a plan isn't going your way, ask yourself: "Am I trying to carry this stone again, or am I rolling it?"

3. **Do Your Best, Leave the Rest:** Committing your work doesn't mean being lazy. It means working with all your heart as if working for the Lord, and then sleeping soundly because the outcome isn't your responsibility.

The great theologian and scientist Blaise Pascal (whom we met in the last chapter) also had a thought on this:

"Our achievements today are but the landing place for our achievements tomorrow."

When we commit our work to God, every "landing place" is part of a staircase He is building for our good and His glory.

A Moment for Reflection

What is the "stone" you are trying to carry today? Is it a financial goal? A relationship you are trying to "fix"? A reputation you are trying to protect?

Feel the weight of it for a second. Now, imagine yourself rolling that weight onto the sturdy, unchanging character of God. He is strong enough to handle the pressure. He is wise enough to know the best outcome. When you roll it over, you might find that your hands are finally free to serve Him with joy instead of stress.

Closing Prayer

Lord, I confess that I often try to establish my own plans. I get tired because I'm trying to carry things that were meant for You. Today, I roll my works onto Your shoulders. I give You my job, my family, and my dreams. Establish my thoughts and lead my steps. I trust that Your plans for me are better than my own. Amen.

References and Further Reading

- **The Life and Faith of George Müller:**
  https://www.christianitytoday.com/history/people/pastorsandpreachers/george-muller.html

- **Lincoln's "Knees" Quote and Faith:**
  https://www.nps.gov/liho/learn/historyculture/lincoln-and-religion.htm

- **Hebrew Word Study: Galal (Commit):**
  https://www.blueletterbible.org/lexicon/h1556/nasb95/wlc/0-1/

- **Blaise Pascal on Achievement:**
  https://www.britannica.com/biography/Blaise-Pascal

Reflection

Take a few minutes to reflect and meditate on what you just read. Write down your thoughts take time to pray and praise God.

_____

_____

_____

_____

_____

_____

_____

_____

_____

_____

_____

_____

_____

_____

_____

_____

_____

Day 15

Conformed

And do not be conformed to this world, but be transformed by the renewing of your mind, so that you may prove what the will of God is, that which is good and acceptable and perfect.
Romans 12:2

This is perhaps one of the most vital commands for a Christian living in the 21st century. After discussing how we commit our works to God, we now look at how we protect our very identity from being "molded" by the world around us. This chapter is about the beautiful, sometimes painful, process of becoming who God actually created you to be.

Chapter 15: Breaking the Mold

Key Verse: *"And do not be conformed to this world, but be transformed by the renewing of your mind, so that you may prove what the will of God is, that which is good and acceptable and perfect."* — **Romans 12:2 (NASB)**

The Pressure of the Press

Have you ever seen a factory machine that makes plastic bottles or metal parts? It uses a "mold." The raw material is poured in, and the machine applies incredible pressure until that material takes the exact shape of the mold. If the mold is shaped like a soda bottle, the plastic has no choice but to become a soda bottle.

The Apostle Paul tells us that the world we live in is trying to do the exact same thing to us. The "world" — the culture, the media, the trends, and the social pressures — is a giant mold. It wants to press you into its shape. It wants you to value what it values: money, power, fame, and looking out for "Number One."

But Paul gives us a counter-command: **Do not be conformed.** In the original language, this carries the idea of "stop allowing yourself to be molded." It is a call to resist the pressure.

Metamorphosis: The Inside-Out Change

If we aren't supposed to be "conformed," what are we supposed to be? Paul uses the word **transformed.** The Greek word is *metamorphoo*. If that sounds familiar, it's because it's where we get our English word "metamorphosis."

Think about a caterpillar. A caterpillar doesn't just put on a butterfly costume. It doesn't just "try harder" to fly. It goes through a complete internal change. Its very nature is rewritten. By the time it leaves the cocoon, it isn't just a "better caterpillar" — it is a brand-new creature.

As Christians, God isn't looking to give us a "makeover." He isn't interested in just fixing a few bad habits. He wants to transform us from the inside out so that we naturally begin to act, think, and love like Jesus.

A Lesson from History: William Tyndale

To understand what it means to refuse to "conform," we can look at William Tyndale, a 16th-century scholar. In his time, the "mold" of the religious and political world said that the Bible should only be in Latin — a language the common people couldn't read. The authorities wanted to keep the "shape" of society exactly as it was, with them in power and the people in the dark.

Tyndale refused to conform to that mold. He believed that even a "boy that driveth the plough" should be able to know the Scripture. He was hunted, he was mocked, and eventually, he was martyred for his work. But because he was transformed by the Word of God, he couldn't stay quiet. He translated the Bible into English, breaking the mold of his era and changing the course of history.

Tyndale once famously said:

"I perceive how that it was impossible to establish the lay people in any truth except the Scripture were plainly laid before their eyes in their mother tongue."

He wasn't shaped by the fears of his time; he was shaped by the truth of God's Word.

The Tool of Transformation: The Renewed Mind

How does this metamorphosis happen? Paul tells us: **"by the renewing of your mind."**

Transformation doesn't happen by sheer willpower. It happens by changing what we put into our minds. If you want to change the output of a computer, you have to change the software. If you want to change the way you live, you have to change the way you think.

When we fill our minds with the "good, acceptable, and perfect" will of God found in the Bible, the old "earthly" software starts to get replaced.

- Instead of thinking, "I need to get revenge," the renewed mind thinks, "God is my defender."

- Instead of thinking, "I am a failure," the renewed mind thinks, "I am a new creation in Christ."

- Instead of thinking, "I need more stuff to be happy," the renewed mind thinks, "God is my portion."

The Story of the Two Statues

Imagine two statues. One is made of cheap clay, and the other is made of solid steel.

If you take a hammer to the clay statue, you can easily dent it and change its shape. It is "conformed" to whatever hits it. But the steel statue is different. It is solid and dense. To change its shape, you would have to melt it down and refine it.

When we don't have a renewed mind, we are like the clay. Every time a new "trend" or a new fear hits us, we get a new dent. We change our values based on who we are hanging out with. But when we are transformed, we become like refined steel. We have an internal strength that comes from God, and the "hammers" of the world can no longer change our shape.

Wisdom from "The Father of Modern Science"

Sir Isaac Newton was a man who revolutionized how we see the world, but he was also a man who refused to let his mind be conformed to a godless view of the universe. While others were beginning to see the world as just a big, cold machine, Newton saw the hand of a Creator.

Newton said:

"This most beautiful system of the sun, planets, and comets, could only proceed from the counsel and dominion of an intelligent and powerful Being."

Newton's mind was renewed by his study of both "God's Book" (the Bible) and "God's Works" (nature). He didn't just follow the crowd; he allowed his transformation to lead him to deeper truths.

How to Resist the Mold Today

Breaking the mold of the world is a daily battle. Here are three ways to stay "transformed" instead of "conformed":

1. **Watch Your "Presses":** Identify the things in your life that are trying to mold you. Is it a certain social media feed? A group of friends who gossip? A TV show that mocks your values? If the pressure is too high, step away.

2. **Soak in the Word:** Just as a dry sponge needs to stay in water to stay soft and useful, our minds need to stay soaked in Scripture to stay "transformable" by God.

3. **The "Proof" Test:** Paul says we are transformed so that we can "prove" what God's will is. Today, ask yourself: "If someone looked at my life, would they see proof that God's way is better than the world's way?"

The great apologist and author G.K. Chesterton once remarked:

"A dead thing can go with the stream, but only a living thing can go against it."

To be conformed is to go with the stream. To be transformed is to be truly alive and to swim toward the source.

A Moment for Reflection

Look in the mirror of your soul today. Whose shape are you taking? Do you look like the culture around you—anxious, angry, and self-absorbed? Or are you starting to look like the "New Creation" God is building?

Don't be discouraged if you still feel like a caterpillar. Transformation takes time. The cocoon isn't a prison; it's a place of growth. Keep renewing your mind, keep choosing the "good and acceptable," and watch as God slowly breaks the old mold to reveal the masterpiece He is making in you.

Closing Prayer

Lord, I feel the pressure of the world trying to push me into its shape every day. I confess that sometimes I give in because it's easier than standing out. Please transform me. Renew my mind with Your truth so that I can see the world through Your eyes. Help me to resist the mold and to live a life that proves Your will is perfect. Amen.

References and Further Reading

- **The Life and Sacrifice of William Tyndale:**
  https://www.christianitytoday.com/history/people/scholarsand scientists/william-tyndale.html

- **Isaac Newton on the Creator:**
  https://www.universetoday.com/38643/isaac-newton-quotes/

- **G.K. Chesterton on Going Against the Stream:**
  https://www.chesterton.org/the-everlasting-man/

- **Word Study: Metamorphoo (Transform):**
  https://biblehub.com/greek/3339.htm

Reflection

Take a few minutes to reflect and meditate on what you just read. Write down your thoughts take time to pray and praise God.

_____

_____

_____

_____

_____

_____

_____

_____

_____

_____

_____

_____

_____

_____

_____

_____

_____

Day 16

Trust in the Lord

Trust in the Lord with all your heart And do not lean on your own understanding. In all your ways acknowledge Him, And He will make your paths straight.
Proverbs 3:5-6

This is one of the most beloved passages in all of Scripture, yet it is also one of the most difficult to live out when life gets "blurry." After talking about being transformed from the inside out, we now look at the foundation that makes that transformation possible: **Trust.**

Chapter 16: The Lean of the Heart

Key Verse: *"Trust in the Lord with all your heart and do not lean on your own understanding. In all your ways acknowledge Him, and He will make your paths straight."* — **Proverbs 3:5-6 (NASB)**

The Problem with "Leaning"

Have you ever walked across a room in total darkness? Even if it's your own living room, you move slowly. You reach out your hands, feeling for the edge of the couch or the doorframe. You are looking for something sturdy to "lean" on so you don't trip over a rug or a stray toy.

In life, we are all leaning on something. We lean on our bank accounts for security. We lean on our health to feel strong. We lean on our own "understanding" — our ability to figure things out — to feel in control. But Solomon, the wisest man who ever lived, warns us that our own understanding is like a toothpick trying to hold up a bowling ball. It's just not strong enough to carry the weight of our lives.

To "trust" in the Hebrew language (*batach*) carries the idea of lying helpless on the ground, face down, totally dependent on someone else. It's the picture of a soldier who has dropped his weapons and is relying entirely on his king for protection.

A Lesson from History: George Washington at Valley Forge

To understand what it looks like to trust God when your "own understanding" says things are hopeless, we can look at George Washington during the winter of 1777 at Valley Forge.

His army was starving, freezing, and dying of disease. They had no shoes, very little food, and the most powerful military in the world was waiting to crush them. By any human "understanding," the American Revolution was over. It was a failure.

But Washington was a man of deep, quiet faith. There are many historical accounts of him retreating into the woods to pray. He wasn't leaning on his military genius or his supplies; he was trusting in "Divine Providence." He acknowledged God in the middle of the snow and the suffering.

Washington once said:

"The hand of Providence has been so conspicuous in all this, that he must be worse than an infidel that lacks faith, and more than wicked that has not gratitude enough to acknowledge his obligations."

Because he trusted God with "all his heart" rather than his own dire circumstances, he was able to lead his men through the winter and eventually to victory. God made the "path straight" even through the crooked, frozen woods of Pennsylvania.

The "All" and the "In All"

Notice the two "alls" in this command.

1. Trust with **all** your heart.

2. **In all** your ways acknowledge Him.

God doesn't want a "weekend custody" of your trust. He doesn't want you to trust Him with your "spiritual life" while you handle your "financial life" or your "dating life" on your own.

Imagine you are going skydiving. You wouldn't say to the instructor, "I trust this parachute 80%." If you don't trust it 100%, you don't jump! Trusting with "all your heart" means you've stopped looking for a backup plan. You are "all in."

The Story of the Tightrope Walker

There is a famous (though likely legendary) story of a great tightrope walker named Blondin who was crossing Niagara Falls. He pushed a wheelbarrow across the thin wire, high above the crashing water, and the crowd cheered.

He turned to a man in the crowd and asked, "Do you believe I can do this?" The man replied, "Of course! I just saw you do it!" Blondin then asked, "Do you trust me?" The man said, "Yes, absolutely." Blondin smiled and said, "Then get in the wheelbarrow."

That is the difference between *belief* and *trust*. Many of us believe God *can* help us, but "trusting with all our heart" means actually getting into the wheelbarrow. It means letting Him take the handles of our lives.

Straightening the Path

The promise at the end of this verse is incredible: **"He will make your paths straight."**

This doesn't mean your life will be easy or that you'll never face a mountain. A "straight path" in the ancient world was a path that had been cleared of big rocks and obstacles so that a traveler could reach their destination without getting lost.

When you stop leaning on your own limited brain and start acknowledging God's wisdom, He begins to clear the path. He opens doors you couldn't see. He closes doors that would have led you into a trap. He gives you a peace that doesn't make sense to your "understanding."

The great scientist and thinker Sir Francis Bacon, who is often called the father of the scientific method, understood the limits of human understanding. He wrote:

"A little philosophy inclineth man's mind to atheism, but depth in philosophy bringeth men's minds about to religion."

Bacon realized that the more you actually "understand" the world, the more you realize you *need* to trust the One who made it.

How to Practice Trust Today

Trusting God is like a muscle; it gets stronger the more you use it. Here are three ways to practice "Proverbs 3 Trust" today:

1. **The "Stop and Lean" Check:** When you feel a surge of anxiety, ask yourself: "What am I leaning on right now? Am I leaning on my own ability to fix this, or am I leaning on God?"

2. **The 10-Second Acknowledgment:** Before you start a meeting, make a phone call, or send an email, take ten seconds to silently say, "Lord, I acknowledge You in this moment. Have Your way." This is how you acknowledge Him in "all your ways."

3. **The "Why" Fast:** For one day, try to stop asking God "Why?" and start saying "Thank You that You know." Trusting God often means being okay with not having an answer as long as you have His hand.

The famous hymn writer Fanny Crosby was blind from the time she was a baby. From a human "understanding," her life was a tragedy. But she wrote over 8,000 hymns because she trusted God with all her heart.

She once said:

"It seemed intended by the blessed providence of God that I should be blind all my life, and I thank Him for the dispensation. If perfect earthly sight were offered me tomorrow I would not accept it."

Fanny Crosby had "straight paths" in her soul because she refused to lean on her own sightless understanding.

A Moment for Reflection

Is there a "crooked path" in your life right now? Maybe it's a relationship that is confusing, a health diagnosis that is scary, or a career path that seems blocked.

Take a deep breath. You don't have to figure it all out today. In fact, God is asking you to *stop* trying to figure it all out on your own. He is asking you to shift your weight. Lean back. Let Him take the lead. When you acknowledge Him — even in the middle of the mess — He takes the responsibility for the destination.

Closing Prayer

Lord, I confess that I am a "leaner." I lean on my own logic, my own hard work, and my own plans. Today, I want to lean on You. I trust You with the things I don't understand. I acknowledge that You are the Boss of my day, my family, and my future. Please make my paths straight and give me the courage to stay in the wheelbarrow. Amen.

References and Further Reading

- **George Washington's Prayer at Valley Forge:** https://www.mountvernon.org/library/digitalhistory/digital-encyclopedia/article/washington-and-religion/

- **The Life and Hymns of Fanny Crosby:** https://www.christianitytoday.com/history/people/poets/fanny-crosby.html

- **Sir Francis Bacon on Faith and Philosophy:** https://plato.stanford.edu/entries/francis-bacon/

- **Hebrew Word Study: Batach (Trust):** https://www.blueletterbible.org/lexicon/h982/nasb95/wlc/0-1/

Reflection

Take a few minutes to reflect and meditate on what you just read. Write down your thoughts take time to pray and praise God.

_____

_____

_____

_____

_____

_____

_____

_____

_____

_____

_____

_____

_____

_____

_____

_____

_____

_____

Day 17

Be Strong

Be strong and courageous, do not be afraid or tremble at them, for the Lord your God is the one who goes with you. He will not fail you or forsake you."
Deuteronomy 31:6

This is a powerful command that acts as a bridge between God's promises and our reality. In this passage, Moses is preparing to hand over leadership to Joshua, and the people are preparing to face giants and fortified cities.

Chapter 17: The Source of True Grit

Key Verse: *"Be strong and courageous, do not be afraid or tremble at them, for the Lord your God is the one who goes with you. He will not fail you or forsake you."* — **Deuteronomy 31:6 (NASB)**

The Command to Be Brave

If you've ever stood at the edge of a high diving board or waited for the results of a medical test, you know what it feels like for your knees to shake. Fear is a natural human reaction to danger. But in the Bible, "courage" isn't the absence of fear; it's the decision that something else is more important than that fear.

When Moses spoke these words to the Israelites, they were standing on the edge of a huge transition. Their leader for the last forty years was leaving. They were about to enter a land full of enemies who were bigger and stronger than they were. By all human logic, they had every reason to "tremble."

But God didn't give them a suggestion to be brave; He gave them a command. And as with every command from God, He provided the reason why they could follow it. The courage didn't have to come from their own muscles or their own confidence. It came from a traveling Companion who never sleeps.

What is Biblical Courage?

In the original Hebrew, the word for "be strong" (*chazaq*) means to fasten onto something, like a person grabbing a handrail during an earthquake. To be "courageous" (*amats*) means to be alert and mentally brave.

True biblical courage isn't "toughing it out" on your own. It is the act of "fastening" yourself to the character of God. It's saying, "I am terrified, but I am holding onto the One who is in control of the thing I'm afraid of."

A Lesson from History: Winston Churchill

While he was a political leader rather than a theologian, Winston Churchill understood the nature of courage better than almost anyone in the 20th century. During the darkest days of World War II, when England stood alone against the Nazi war machine, the people were filled with fear.

Churchill didn't ignore the danger, but he commanded a spirit of courage in the people. He knew that if the mind gave way to fear, the battle was already lost.

Churchill once said:

"Courage is rightly esteemed the first of human qualities... because it is the quality which guarantees all others."

For the Christian, courage is what "guarantees" our ability to do justice, love mercy, and walk humbly. Without courage, we will tuck our faith away the moment it becomes unpopular or difficult.

The Story of David and the Giant

We see the perfect illustration of Deuteronomy 31:6 in the story of David and Goliath in **1 Samuel 17**.

The entire Israeli army was "trembling" (just like the warning in our key verse). Why? Because they were looking at the giant. They were measuring Goliath's height against their own height. But when young David walked onto the battlefield, he wasn't measuring Goliath against himself. He was measuring Goliath against God.

David said to the giant in **1 Samuel 17:45 (NASB)**: *"You come to me with a sword, a spear, and a javelin, but I come to you in the name of the Lord of hosts..."*

David was strong and courageous because he knew who was "going with him." He knew that the giant was a speck of dust compared to the Creator of the universe. Courage is simply a matter of who you are looking at.

"He Will Not Fail You"

The second half of our key verse is the "anchor" for our courage: **"He will not fail you or forsake you."**

The world fails us all the time. People let us down. Economies crash. Health fades. But God is promising a 100% success rate on His presence. He might not always take away the giant, and He might not always make the path easy, but He will never — not for one second — leave the room.

The great explorer Sir Ernest Shackleton, who led an Antarctic expedition that became a legendary story of survival, once spoke about this "presence." After his ship was crushed by ice and his men had to trek across frozen mountains, Shackleton noted that he often felt like there was "another person" walking with them, guiding them through the impossible cold.

As a man of faith, he recognized that when you are at the end of your own strength, God's presence becomes more "conspicuous" (visible).

Why We Can Stop Trembling

To "tremble" means to lose heart or to be shattered by fear. We tremble when we think the outcome depends entirely on us.

- You don't have to tremble about your **finances** because the One who owns the "cattle on a thousand hills" goes with you.

- You don't have to tremble about **loneliness** because the Friend who sticks closer than a brother will not forsake you.

- You don't have to tremble about the **future** because He is already there, preparing the way.

As the famous American President Theodore Roosevelt said:

"It is not the critic who counts... The credit belongs to the man who is actually in the arena, whose face is marred by dust and sweat and blood; who strives valiantly."

God is calling you into the "arena" of your life today. He knows it's dusty. He knows it's hard. But He is in the arena with you.

How to Practice Courage Today

Courage is a choice we make one minute at a time. Here are three ways to be "strong and courageous" this week:

1. **The "Who is Bigger?" Test:** When a problem keeps you awake at night, visualize that problem standing next to God. See how small the problem looks in His hand.

2. **Speak the Promise:** When you feel yourself starting to "tremble" or feel anxious, say the words out loud: "The Lord goes with me. He will not fail me." There is power in hearing the truth spoken.

3. **Take One Small Step:** Courage doesn't mean jumping across a canyon. It often means just taking one step forward when you really want to run away. Do the one thing you've been avoiding because you're afraid.

The great "Prince of Preachers," Charles Spurgeon, once said:

"I have learned to kiss the wave that throws me against the Rock of Ages."

If the scary things in your life (the "waves") force you to grab onto God (the "Rock") more tightly, then you are actually becoming stronger through the struggle.

A Moment for Reflection

What is the "giant" in your life right now? What is the thing that makes your heart beat a little too fast when you think about it?

God is looking at you right now, not with disappointment because you're afraid, but with an invitation. He's saying, "I'm here. I'm not going anywhere. Fasten yourself to Me. Let's walk into this together." You don't need to find more strength inside yourself; you just need to lean on the infinite strength of the One who promised to never leave you.

Closing Prayer

Lord, I thank You that You don't ask me to be brave on my own. I confess that I often tremble when I look at the giants in my life. Please help me to fasten my heart to Your promises today. Remind me that You are walking beside me in every meeting, every hard conversation, and every lonely moment. I choose to be strong and courageous because You are faithful. Amen.

References and Further Reading

- **The Meaning of Strength and Courage (Hebrew Word Study):** https://www.blueletterbible.org/lexicon/h2388/nasb95/wlc/0-1/

- **Winston Churchill on Courage and Leadership:** https://winthrop.edu/leadership/churchill-quotes.aspx

- **Ernest Shackleton and the "Third Man" Factor:** https://www.pbs.org/wgbh/nova/shackleton/1914/

- **Theodore Roosevelt's "Man in the Arena" Speech:** https://www.theodorerooseveltcenter.org/Learn-About-TR/TR-Encyclopedia/Culture-and-Society/Man-in-the-Arena.aspx

Reflection

Take a few minutes to reflect and meditate on what you just read. Write down your thoughts take time to pray and praise God.

_____

_____

_____

_____

_____

_____

_____

_____

_____

_____

_____

_____

_____

_____

_____

_____

_____

_____

Day 18

Love of Money

Make sure that your character is free from the love of money, being content with what you have; for He Himself has said, "I will never desert you, nor will I ever forsake you,"
Hebrews 13:5

This is a vital topic for the modern believer. We live in a world that measures success by a bank balance and security by an investment portfolio. But the author of Hebrews points us toward a different kind of wealth—one that doesn't fluctuate with the stock market.

Chapter 18: The Currency of Contentment

Key Verse: *"Make sure that your character is free from the love of money, being content with what you have; for He Himself has said, 'I will never desert you, nor will I ever forsake you.'"* — **Hebrews 13:5 (NASB)**

The Root of the Restlessness

Have you ever noticed that "enough" always seems to be just a little bit more than what you currently have? If you make fifty thousand dollars a year, you think sixty thousand would make you feel secure. If you have a two-bedroom house, you think a three-bedroom would finally give you the space you need.

The Bible doesn't say that *money* is the problem. Money is just a tool, like a hammer or a shovel. The problem is the **love of money**. In the original Greek, the word used here is *aphilargyros*, which literally means "not a lover of silver." It describes a person who isn't constantly chasing the next dollar to find happiness.

When we love money, we are actually asking money to do something it was never designed to do: provide us with peace, identity, and a sense of "okay-ness."

The Shadow of "More"

The "love of money" is a cruel master because it can never be satisfied. It's like drinking salt water to quench your thirst; the more you drink, the thirstier you get. This leads to a life of "conforming" to the world's hustle and losing our "straight paths".

A Lesson from History: John Wesley

John Wesley, the 18th-century theologian and founder of Methodism, had a very famous rule regarding money: *"Gain all you can, save all you can, and give all you can."*

Wesley was a man who lived out Hebrews 13:5 to the letter. As his income rose throughout his life because of the sale of his books, he didn't raise his standard of living. When he earned 30 pounds a year, he lived on 28 and gave away 2. When his earnings rose to 60, 90, and eventually 120 pounds, he *still* lived on 28 pounds and gave the rest away.

He was "free from the love of money" because he viewed himself as a manager of God's funds, not the owner. He famously said:

"Money never stays with me. It would burn me if it did. I throw it out of my hands as soon as possible, lest it should find a way into my heart."

Wesley understood that the only way to keep money from owning you is to keep it moving toward others.

The Secret of Contentment

The verse gives us the "antidote" to the love of money: **"being content with what you have."**

Contentment isn't about being lazy or not having goals. It's about a "settled-ness" in the soul. It's saying, "If God gives me more, I will use it for His glory. If He doesn't, I already have everything I truly need."

How is that possible? The author of Hebrews tells us why we can be content: **"For He Himself has said, 'I will never desert you, nor will I ever forsake you.'"**

This is the ultimate promise. We chase money because we are afraid of being deserted. We are afraid of being hungry, alone, or forgotten. But God says that *He* is our security. You can lose your job, your savings, and your house, but you cannot lose the presence of God. If you have the Creator of the universe walking beside you, you are the wealthiest person on the planet.

The Story of the Rich Fool

Jesus told a sobering story in **Luke 12:15–21** about a man whose "character" was not free from the love of money. The man had a massive harvest — so big that his barns couldn't hold it.

Instead of being content and sharing the extra, he said, "I will tear down my barns and build bigger ones!" He thought his "more" would allow him to "eat, drink, and be merry" for years. But God called him a fool, and that very night his life was over.

The man spent his life building a "safety net" made of grain and gold, only to find out it couldn't catch him when he fell into eternity. He was rich in the world's eyes, but he was a pauper in the eyes of God.

Wisdom from the "Steel Magnate"

Andrew Carnegie was once the richest man in the world. He spent the first half of his life making money and the second half giving it all away to libraries and universities. Even a man with his vast wealth realized that money itself had no power to improve the soul.

Carnegie wrote:

"The amassing of wealth is one of the worst species of idolatry. No idol more debasing than the worship of money."

Carnegie saw that even for the ultra-wealthy, the "love" of it was a trap. He realized that a man who dies with millions of dollars of unspent wealth "dies disgraced." He was searching for the "contentment" that Hebrews 13:5 says only comes from God's presence.

How to Practice "Money Freedom" Today

Living free from the love of money doesn't mean you have to sell everything you own today, but it does mean you need to "loosen your grip."

1. **The "Presence" Reminder:** When you feel a pang of financial anxiety, stop and repeat the promise: "He will never desert me." Remind your heart that your bank balance is not your Shepherd.

2. **Practice "Giving First":** One of the best ways to prove you don't love money is to give some away as soon as you get it. This "breaks the power" of the dollar over your heart.

3. **The "Enough" Prayer:** Look around your home today and find three things you are tempted to "upgrade." Pray and thank God for the ones you already have. Tell Him, "This is enough because I have You."

As the Great Reformer Martin Luther once said:

"There are three conversions necessary: the conversion of the heart, then the mind, and finally the purse."

We cannot truly say we are "transformed" (Chapter 15) or "trusting" (Chapter 16) if our relationship with our "purse" hasn't changed.

A Moment for Reflection

If someone looked at your bank statement and your calendar, would they see someone who is "free" or someone who is "captured" by the pursuit of more?

Money is a wonderful servant but a terrible god. Today, take a deep breath and remember that the King of Kings has committed Himself to your well-being. He has promised never to leave you. You don't have to scramble or worry or hoard. You can be content, because your greatest Treasure is already yours.

Closing Prayer

Lord, I confess that I often look to money to make me feel safe and significant. Please forgive me for loving the gift more than the Giver. Help me to be truly content with what I have today. Remind my anxious heart that You will never desert me or forsake me. May my character be defined by Your presence, not my possessions. Amen.

References and Further Reading

- **John Wesley on Money and Giving:**
  https://www.resourceumc.org/en/content/john-wesley-on-money

- **The Gospel of Wealth by Andrew Carnegie:**
  https://www.carnegie.org/about/our-history/gospelofwealth/

- **Martin Luther's "Three Conversions":**
  https://www.lutheranworld.org/content/martin-luther-quotes

- **Word Study: Aphilargyros (Free from Love of Money):**
  https://biblehub.com/greek/866.htm

Reflection

Take a few minutes to reflect and meditate on what you just read. Write down your thoughts take time to pray and praise God.

_____

_____

_____

_____

_____

_____

_____

_____

_____

_____

_____

_____

_____

_____

_____

_____

_____

Day 19

Flee

Now flee from youthful lusts and pursue righteousness, faith, love and peace, with those who call on the Lord from a pure heart.
2 Timothy 2:22

This chapter brings us to a command that feels almost out of place in our modern world of "standing your ground" and "facing your fears." We've spent a lot of time talking about being strong and courageous, but the Bible is also very practical. It tells us that there are some battles you don't win by fighting—you win them by running away.

Chapter 19: The Wisdom of the Exit

Key Verse: *"Now flee from youthful lusts and pursue righteousness, faith, love and peace, with those who call on the Lord from a pure heart."* — **2 Timothy 2:22** **(NASB)**

The Two-Way Motion

Have you ever seen a "One Way" sign on a busy city street? If you try to drive the wrong way, you're headed for a disaster. The Christian life has its own set of "One Way" signs, and in this verse, Paul gives Timothy—a young leader—a clear set of traffic directions.

There is a "from" and a "to." We are told to move *away* from one thing and *toward* another.

The command to **"flee"** (the Greek word *pheuge*) is intense. It's where we get our word "fugitive." It doesn't mean to mosey away or to slowly back out of the room. It means to run as if your life depends on it. It's the action of someone who looks behind them, sees a fire, and realizes they need to get out immediately.

Why We Run

Why would a "strong and courageous" Christian (as we discussed in Chapter 10) ever be told to run?

It's because our "youthful lusts" — which aren't just about physical desires, but can include pride, a craving for constant entertainment, or a hot temper — are like a virus. If you stay in the room with a virus, you're likely to catch it, no matter how "strong" you think your immune system is.

True courage includes the humility to admit, "I am not strong enough to sit in this temptation and play with it." Sometimes, the most "mighty" thing you can do for your faith is to find the nearest exit.

A Lesson from History: George Washington's "Fabian" Strategy

We often think of great generals as people who always charge forward. But during the American Revolution, George Washington became famous for a strategy of "strategic retreat."

He knew that his army was often outmatched by the British. If he stayed and fought every battle "toe-to-toe," the American cause would have been crushed in a month. So, Washington became a master of "fleeing." He would strike, then pull his troops back into the hills where the enemy couldn't reach them.

Washington once wrote:

"We should on all occasions avoid a general Action, or put anything to the Risque, unless compelled by a necessity, into which we ought never to be drawn."

Washington knew that to "pursue" victory in the long run, he had to "flee" certain battles in the short run. He wasn't being a coward; he was being a strategist. In the same way, Paul is telling Timothy: "Don't risk your soul for the sake of proving how strong you are. Flee the temptation so you can live to pursue the righteousness."

What We Pursue

If we just ran away from things, we would eventually get tired and stop. That's why Paul gives us a second command: **Pursue.** You can't just leave a vacuum in your heart. If you stop "fleeing" from the bad stuff but don't start "pursuing" the good stuff, the bad stuff will eventually catch back up to you. We are told to chase after:

- **Righteousness:** Doing what is right in God's eyes.

- **Faith:** Trusting God more (as we saw in Chapter 9).

- **Love:** Seeking the best for others.

- **Peace:** Living in harmony with God and people.

The Story of Joseph in Egypt

The most famous "flee-er" in the Bible is Joseph. In **Genesis 39**, Joseph was a successful manager in the house of an Egyptian official named Potiphar. Potiphar's wife tried to seduce him day after day.

Joseph didn't try to sit her down for a theological debate. He didn't try to "reform" her. He didn't even try to explain why it was wrong more than once. When she finally grabbed him by his coat, the Bible says he **"left his garment in her hand and fled, and went outside" (Genesis 39:12, NASB).**

Joseph lost his coat, his job, and eventually his freedom (for a while) because he ran. But he kept his integrity and his relationship with God. He understood that his soul was worth more than his reputation.

The Power of the "Circle"

Paul adds one more vital instruction: Do this **"with those who call on the Lord from a pure heart."**

Running is hard. Chasing righteousness is even harder. You aren't meant to be a "solo fugitive." You need a group of people running in the same direction. When you have friends who are also pursuing love and peace, they can grab your arm when you start to slow down, and you can encourage them when they feel like turning back.

The great Christian author and apologist C.S. Lewis had his own "running circle" called The Inklings. This group of writers (including J.R.R. Tolkien) met regularly to pursue excellence in their work and their faith.

Lewis once said:

"Friendship is unnecessary, like philosophy, like art... It has no survival value; rather it is one of those things which give value to survival."

When you "flee" the world's lusts, you need those friendships to give your "pursuit" value and joy.

How to "Flee" Today

Fleeing isn't just about physical running; it's about mental and digital running, too.

1. **The "Unfollow" Button:** If a certain social media account consistently makes you feel lustful, envious, or angry, "flee" from it by hitting unfollow. Don't try to "manage" the temptation — remove it.

2. **Change the Environment:** If you know that going to a certain place or hanging out with a certain crowd always leads you to make bad choices, make a "Strategic Retreat" and find a new place to be.

3. **The "Pursuit" Partner:** Identify one person this week you can talk to about your faith. Ask them, "How can we chase after peace and love together?"

For the Christian, one of our greatest "victories" is winning the battle over our own impulses by having the wisdom to walk away from them.

A Moment for Reflection

Is there something you've been trying to "fight" that you really should be "fleeing"? Maybe it's a grudge you keep revisiting, a website you keep clicking on, or a "youthful" need to always be right.

Stop trying to prove how strong you are. God has already given you an out. Turn your back on the fire and start running toward the "righteousness, faith, love, and peace" that is waiting for you. And as you run, look around — you'll find that you aren't running alone.

Closing Prayer

Lord, I thank You for Your practical wisdom. I confess that sometimes I am too proud to run. I think I can handle temptation on my own, and I end up getting burned. Please give me the humility to flee when I need to and the endurance to pursue You with all my heart. Surround me with friends who will run toward Your peace with me. Amen.

References and Further Reading

- **George Washington's Fabian Strategy:** https://www.mountvernon.org/library/digitalhistory/digital-encyclopedia/article/fabian-strategy/

- **The Story of Joseph and Potiphar's Wife:** https://www.biblegateway.com/resources/commentary/IVP-OT/Gen.39.1-Gen.39.23

- **C.S. Lewis and the Inklings:** https://www.cslewis.com/the-inklings/

- **Word Study: Pheuge (Flee):** https://biblehub.com/greek/5343.htm

Reflection

Take a few minutes to reflect and meditate on what you just read. Write down your thoughts take time to pray and praise God.

_____

_____

_____

_____

_____

_____

_____

_____

_____

_____

_____

_____

_____

_____

_____

_____

_____

Day 20

Shine Your Light

Let your light shine before men in such a way that they may see your good works, and glorify your Father who is in heaven.
Matthew 5:16

This chapter takes us from the "fleeing" and "pursuing" of our private lives and places us directly on the world's stage. After learning how to protect our hearts, we now explore how to project God's heart. In the middle of His most famous sermon, Jesus gives us a command that defines our purpose in a dark world.

Chapter 20: The Unveiled Flame

Key Verse: *"Let your light shine before men in such a way that they may see your good works, and glorify your Father who is in heaven."* — **Matthew 5:16** **(NASB)**

The Purpose of a Lamp

Have you ever been in a house during a total power outage? The darkness is heavy and disorienting. You fumble for a flashlight or a candle. When you finally strike a match, that tiny flame becomes the most important thing in the room. You don't strike a match and then put it under a bucket; that would be a waste of the match and the fuel.

Jesus tells us that as His followers, we are the "light of the world." But notice that He doesn't just say "be light." He gives an active command: **"Let your light shine."**

This implies that it is possible to be a Christian and yet keep your light hidden. We hide our light when we are quiet about our faith because we're afraid of what people think. We hide it when we act exactly like the rest of the world. Jesus is saying that the world is in a "power outage," and your life is the candle that is meant to help people see.

Good Works: The Fuel for the Flame

How does this light actually shine? Is it by shouting at people or carrying a megaphone? Jesus says it happens through our **"good works."**

In the original language, the word for "good" here doesn't just mean "moral" or "not bad." It means "beautiful," "attractive," or "excellent." Our lives should be so beautiful and our actions so kind that people can't help but notice.

When you help a neighbor, when you are honest when it costs you money, or when you show grace to someone who doesn't deserve it, you are "shining." Your good works are the beams of light that cut through the darkness of a cynical world.

A Lesson from History: Florence Nightingale's Lamp

We met Florence Nightingale earlier in this book, but she fits perfectly here as well. During the Crimean War, she became known as "The Lady with the Lamp."

At night, when the doctors had gone to bed and the hospital wards were dark and filled with the groans of wounded soldiers, Florence would walk the hallways with a small Turkish lantern. The light from her lamp didn't just help her see where she was walking; it brought hope to the men. The sight of that tiny flame meant that someone cared, that someone was watching, and that they weren't alone in the dark.

She once said:

"I am of certain convinced that the greatest help, if not the only help, we can give to those who are suffering is to be ourselves what we would have them be."

Florence didn't just talk about compassion; she "shone" it through her work. Her "good works" were so bright that they eventually changed the laws of England and the practice of medicine worldwide.

The Ultimate Goal: Reflecting the Father

There is a very important detail at the end of our key verse. We aren't shining so that people will say, "Wow, look how great you are!" We shine so that they will **"glorify your Father who is in heaven."**

A good mirror doesn't draw attention to itself; it shows you the person standing in front of it. A window is most effective when it is so clean you don't even see the glass — you only see the view outside.

As Christians, we are like the moon. The moon has no light of its own; it is just a big, gray rock. But when it faces the sun, it reflects the sun's light so brightly that it can guide a traveler through the night. Our goal is to stay so close to the "Son" that people see His reflection in us and realize how great He is.

The Story of the City on a Hill

Just before our key verse, Jesus says in **Matthew 5:14 (NASB)**: "*A city set on a hill cannot be hidden.*" In the ancient world, cities were often built on hilltops for safety. At night, the oil lamps in the houses would merge together to create a glow that could be seen from miles away. A traveler lost in the wilderness could look up, see that glow, and know which way to walk to find safety and a warm meal.

When we live out the commands of God — when we seek justice, love mercy, and walk humbly — we become that "city." We provide a "homing signal" for people who are lost in the darkness of addiction, depression, or hopelessness. They see the "glow" of our community and realize there is a better way to live.

Wisdom from a "Liberator of Minds"

Frederick Douglass, the great abolitionist and statesman, was a man whose light shone through some of the darkest periods of American history. He understood that faith without "shining" works was empty.

Douglass once remarked:

"I would agree with any person to do right, and with no person to do wrong."

By consistently doing what was "right" and "beautiful" even when it was dangerous, Douglass forced a whole nation to look at the "Father in heaven" and ask if they were living according to His light. His light was too bright to be ignored by the "bucket" of slavery.

How to Shine Your Light Today

Shining isn't about being perfect; it's about being visible. Here are three ways to "unveil" your flame this week:

1. **The "Silent Sermon":** Find a task at work or at home that nobody wants to do and do it with a cheerful heart. Your attitude is a light that people will notice.

2. **The Encouragement Beam:** We live in a world of "dark" words—criticism and complaining. Shine your light by being the one person who speaks life and encouragement into someone's day.

3. **The Credit Shift:** When someone praises you for a job well done, don't just say "thanks." Say something like, "Thank you! I've been asking God for help with this, and I'm so glad it turned out well." That "shifts" the glory to the Father.

The great scientist and Christian, Michael Faraday, who discovered electromagnetic induction, used to say that even the simplest candle was a wonder of God's creation. He said:

"All this is a dream. Still, examine it by a few experiments. Nothing is too wonderful to be true, if it be consistent with the laws of nature."

Faraday used his scientific "light" to show the wonders of God. He believed that the more we "examine" the truth, the more we see the glory of the Creator.

A Moment for Reflection

Is your "lamp" under a bucket today? Are you so worried about "fitting in" that nobody even knows you follow Jesus?

The world doesn't need more people who blend into the shadows. It needs people who are brave enough to be "bright." Your light doesn't have to be a massive spotlight; sometimes a tiny candle is all it takes to change the atmosphere of a room. Today, look for one "beautiful work" you can do that points people toward the Father.

Closing Prayer

Lord, thank You for putting Your light inside of me. I confess that sometimes I hide my faith because I'm afraid of being different. Please take the "bucket" off my life. Help me to do good and beautiful works today — not so people will think I'm great, but so they will see how wonderful You are. Let my life be a lighthouse for someone who is lost in the dark. Amen.

References and Further Reading

- **Florence Nightingale: The Lady with the Lamp:**
  https://www.florence-nightingale.co.uk/the-crimean-war/

- **Frederick Douglass on Faith and Right Action:**
  https://www.nps.gov/frdo/learn/historyculture/index.htm

- **Michael Faraday's "Chemical History of a Candle":**
  https://www.britannica.com/biography/Michael-Faraday

- **Word Study: Kalos (Good/Beautiful):**
  https://biblehub.com/greek/2570.htm

Reflection

Take a few minutes to reflect and meditate on what you just read. Write down your thoughts take time to pray and praise God.

_____

_____

_____

_____

_____

_____

_____

_____

_____

_____

_____

_____

_____

_____

_____

_____

_____

_____

Day 21

Cast Your Burden

Cast your burden upon the Lord and He will sustain you; He will never allow the righteous to be shaken.
Psalm 55:22

This chapter takes the beautiful concept of "rolling" our works onto God and applies it to the heavy, emotional weights we carry. In the middle of a poem written by a man who felt betrayed and overwhelmed, we find a command that offers true rest for our souls.

Chapter 21: The Great Exchange

Key Verse: *"Cast your burden upon the Lord and He will sustain you; He will never allow the righteous to be shaken."* — **Psalm 55:22 (NASB)**

The Weight of the World

Have you ever tried to carry too many grocery bags from the car into the house in one trip? Your fingers turn red, your arms start to shake, and you're desperately looking for a counter where you can just drop everything.

Life can feel exactly like those grocery bags. We carry the burden of financial stress, the weight of a broken relationship, or the heavy "bags" of grief and anxiety. We try to be strong, we try to power through, but eventually, our "fingers" start to slip.

King David, who wrote this Psalm, knew this feeling well. When he wrote these words, he wasn't sitting in a peaceful palace; he was being hunted by enemies and had been betrayed by his own close friend.

He felt like his heart was "in anguish" (**Psalm 55:4**). In that moment of absolute exhaustion, he realized he had two choices: keep carrying the weight until it crushed him, or follow the command to **cast it.**

The Physics of Casting

The word "cast" in the original Hebrew (*shalak*) isn't a gentle suggestion. It means to throw, to hurl, or to fling something away from yourself. It's the action of a person who realizes they are holding something dangerous — like a hot coal or a snake — and they get rid of it as fast as they can.

When we "cast" our burdens, we aren't just politely mentioning them to God in a prayer. We are intentionally flinging the *responsibility* for that burden onto Him. We are saying, "Lord, this is too heavy for me. I am throwing it into Your lap. It is Your problem now."

A Lesson from History: George Müller's Secret

We met George Müller earlier in this book as the man who cared for thousands of orphans. While we talked about his "works," he is also a master-class in "casting burdens."

One night, Müller was told that the orphanage had no milk for the children's breakfast the next morning. A man with thousands of hungry children depending on him would naturally be crushed by the "burden" of that reality. Most of us wouldn't be able to sleep!

But Müller had learned to "cast." He prayed, told God about the need, and then — this is the key — he went to sleep. He refused to stay awake and "worry" about the milk. He had thrown the burden onto the Lord.

Müller once wrote:

"The first thing to be concerned about was not how much I might serve the Lord, but how I might get my soul into a happy state, and how my inner man might be nourished."

He knew that he couldn't serve the children if he was being crushed by a burden he wasn't meant to carry. By morning, as we noted before, the milk arrived. God sustained him because Müller let go of the weight.

The Promise of Sustainability

Notice the promise that follows the command: **"and He will sustain you."** It doesn't say "He will immediately take the problem away." Sometimes He does, but often, the problem remains while *we* are changed. To "sustain" means to nourish, to provide for, and to hold up.

Think of a bridge. The weight of the cars (the burdens) doesn't disappear when they drive across it. But the pillars underneath the bridge are so strong that they "sustain" the bridge so it doesn't collapse under the weight.

When you cast your burden on the Lord, He becomes the pillars under your soul. The weight is still there, but He is the one feeling the pressure, not you.

The Story of the Two Porters

There is an old story about a man walking down a dusty road, struggling under a massive, heavy crate on his shoulders. A man in a horse-drawn wagon pulls up and offers him a ride.

The traveler climbs into the wagon, but he keeps the heavy crate on his shoulders! The driver looks back and says, "My friend, why don't you put the crate down? The wagon can carry both you and your burden."

Many of us do this with God. We "get in the wagon" by trusting Him for our salvation, but we keep the "crate" of our daily worries on our own backs.

We are in the wagon, but we aren't resting. God is saying, "Put the crate down. I've got the wagon, and I've got the horse. I can handle the weight."

Wisdom from a "Common Sense" Scientist

Benjamin Franklin, whom we've visited before, was a man of action and immense responsibility. He dealt with the "burdens" of forming a new nation. He realized that a mind cluttered with worry was a mind that couldn't think clearly.

Franklin once said:

"Be at war with your vices, at peace with your neighbors, and let every new year find you a better man."

He understood that to be "at peace," one had to manage the internal world. For the Christian, that peace comes from the realization that we don't have to be the "General" of our own lives. We have a Commander-in-Chief who takes the responsibility for the outcome.

How to "Cast" Your Burdens Today

Casting is a physical act of the will. Here are three ways to do it today:

1. **The "Physical Flings":** When you feel a burden of anxiety, literally open your hands and move your arms as if you are throwing something away from you toward heaven. Tell God, "I'm casting this [name the worry] onto You right now."

2. **The "Sustain" Log:** At the end of the day, write down one thing that was hard and one way God "sustained" you through it. Maybe it was a word of encouragement from a friend or just the strength to get through a meeting.

3. **The "Nightly Deposit":** Before you close your eyes, say: "Lord, I am going to sleep. I cannot solve this problem while I sleep, so I am leaving it in Your hands. I'll check back with You in the morning."

As the great 19th-century preacher Dwight L. Moody said:

"Trust in yourself, and you are doomed to disappointment; trust in your money, and you may have it taken from you; but trust in God, and you will never be confounded in time or eternity."

If you trust God with the burden, you won't be "confounded" or shaken, because the Rock of Ages doesn't move.

A Moment for Reflection

What are you still carrying that you should have dropped miles ago? Is it the guilt of a past mistake? The fear of a future "what-if"?

You weren't built to carry that weight. Your "shoulders" were designed for worship, not for the crushing pressure of being your own god. Today, take that heavy sack of groceries and "cast" it. Feel the blood come back into your fingers. Feel the strength of the Lord rise up beneath you. He is ready to sustain you, but you have to let go of the bag first.

Closing Prayer

Lord, I am tired of carrying these burdens. I confess that I've been trying to be strong enough to handle it all on my own. Right now, I hurl my worries, my fears, and my "what-ifs" onto You. Thank You for Your promise to sustain me and for being the foundation that cannot be shaken. I'm putting my crate down in Your wagon. Amen.

References and Further Reading

- **George Müller on Prayer and Faith:**
  https://www.mullers.org/george-muller

- **Benjamin Franklin's Rules for Life:**
  https://www.fi.edu/en/science-and-education/benjamin-franklin/virtues

- **D.L. Moody's Sermons on Trust:**
  https://www.moody.edu/about/our-history/dwight-lyman-moody/

- **Word Study: Shalak (Cast):**
  https://www.blueletterbible.org/lexicon/h7993/nasb95/wlc/0-1/

Reflection

Take a few minutes to reflect and meditate on what you just read. Write down your thoughts take time to pray and praise God.

_____

_____

_____

_____

_____

_____

_____

_____

_____

_____

_____

_____

_____

_____

_____

_____

_____

Day 22

Love One Another

A new commandment I give to you, that you love one another, even as I have loved you, that you also love one another.
John 13:34

This chapter brings us to what Jesus called a "new" commandment. We have talked about justice, mercy, humility, and trust—all of which are vital. But here, on the night before He went to the cross, Jesus gave His followers a command that acts as the "uniform" for the Christian life. It's not just about who we are, but how we treat the person standing right in front of us.

Chapter 22: The Christian Uniform

Key Verse: *"A new commandment I give to you, that you love one another, even as I have loved you, that you also love one another."* — **John 13:34 (NASB)**

The New Standard

Have you ever seen a sports team take the field? You know exactly who belongs to which team because of the jerseys they wear. The colors and the logos tell the world, "I belong to this group."

In the ancient world, people were identified by their clothes, their language, or their tribe. But Jesus told His disciples that they were going to have a different kind of "uniform." It wouldn't be a specific robe or a certain style of hair. It would be the way they loved each other.

But wait—wasn't "love your neighbor" already an old rule? Why did Jesus call this a **"new commandment"**? The "newness" isn't in the word *love*; it's in the *standard* of that love. Before, the rule was "love your neighbor as yourself." But Jesus raised the bar. He said, **"even as I have loved you."**

That changes everything. We are no longer the measure of our own love. Jesus is.

A Love That Stoops

To understand how Jesus loved, we only have to look at what happened just a few minutes before He gave this command. In the same chapter, **John 13:1–17**, we see the King of the Universe wrap a towel around His waist, get down on His knees, and wash the dirty, dusty feet of His disciples—including the feet of Judas, the man who was about to betray Him.

Jesus' love isn't a "feeling" or a "vibe." It is a deliberate choice to serve. It is a love that stoops down to meet the needs of others, even when they don't deserve it.

A Lesson from History: The "Common" Love of William Wilberforce

We met William Wilberforce earlier in the book as a champion of justice, but his life was also a masterpiece of "loving one another." Even as he fought big political battles, he was known for a personal, tender love for the individuals in his life.

He lived by the idea that every human being was made in the image of God and deserved to be loved "as Christ loved us." He spent his own fortune helping the poor, and he was known for his extreme kindness to his political enemies.

Wilberforce once said:

"True Christian benevolence is not a weak and listless thing... it is a principle of vigorous and active nature, which leads us to do good to all men, and especially to those who are of the household of faith."

He understood that if he wanted to change the world's laws, he first had to live by the "New Commandment" in his own living room and in the halls of Parliament.

The Power of "One Another"

The Bible contains over fifty "one another" commands. We are told to pray for one another, encourage one another, bear one another's burdens, and forgive one another. But "love one another" is the umbrella that covers them all.

When we love as Jesus loved, we stop asking, "What can this person do for me?" and start asking, "How can I lay down my life for this person?" Laying down your life doesn't always mean dying; usually, it means laying down your time, your "right" to be angry, or your preference for how an afternoon should go.

The Story of the Two Brothers

There is an old legend about two brothers who farmed neighboring land. One was married with many children, and the other was single. At the end of a harvest, the single brother thought, "My brother has a large family to feed; he needs more grain than I do." So, in the middle of the night, he secretly carried sacks of grain to his brother's barn.

Meanwhile, the married brother thought, "My brother is alone; he has no children to care for him in his old age. He needs to save more than I do." So, he secretly carried sacks of grain to his single brother's barn.

One night, they bumped into each other in the dark, carrying their sacks. They realized what was happening, dropped their grain, and embraced. The legend says that God looked down and said, "On this spot, I will build my Temple."

While this is just a story, it captures the heart of John 13:34. When we are so busy looking out for "one another" that we forget to worry about ourselves, we create a place where God's presence is clearly seen.

Wisdom from the "Father of Modern Science"

Sir Isaac Newton, whom we've seen as a giant of intellect, was also a man who thought deeply about the law of love. He saw the physical laws of the universe (like gravity) as a reflection of the spiritual laws of God.

Newton once wrote:

"He who loves not his brother, whom he hath seen, how can he love God, whom he hath not seen?"

Newton realized that our love for the people we see every day is the "test" of our love for the God we cannot see. If we can't be kind to the person at the grocery store or the family member who is annoying us, our "theology" doesn't mean much.

How to Wear the Uniform Today

Putting on the "love" uniform takes practice. Here are three ways to "love one another" this week:

1. **The "Stoop" Challenge:** Look for one "lowly" task this week that you would usually expect someone else to do—washing the dishes, taking out the trash, or cleaning up a mess you didn't make. Do it as an act of love for "one another."

2. **The Forgiveness Sprint:** Is there someone you are holding a grudge against? Jesus loved us while we were still sinners. "Love one another" means letting go of that "debt" today, not because they apologized, but because Jesus let go of yours.

3. **Active Listening:** One of the greatest ways to love someone is to give them your full, undivided attention. Put your phone away and truly listen to someone's heart for ten minutes.

For the Christian, love isn't just "charity"—it is a command from our King. It is the way we show the world that Jesus is real.

A Moment for Reflection

Think about the person in your life who is the hardest to love. Maybe they are critical, ungrateful, or just plain difficult.

Now, look at the Cross. Jesus loved you when you were at your worst. He didn't wait for you to "get it together" before He stooped to wash your soul.

Today, you have a chance to wear the "uniform." You have a chance to show that person a love they didn't earn. When you do that, you aren't just being a "nice person" — you are fulfilling the New Commandment. You are letting the world see the Father through you.

Closing Prayer

Lord, thank You for the way You have loved me. I am overwhelmed by the thought of You washing the feet of Your disciples. Please forgive me for being selfish and for only loving people who are easy to love. Help me to put on the "uniform" of love today. Give me the strength to stoop, the heart to serve, and the grace to forgive. May the world see You through the way I treat others. Amen.

References and Further Reading

- **William Wilberforce on Christian Benevolence:**
  https://www.williamwilberforce.org/

- **The "One Another" Commands in Scripture:**
  https://www.biblegateway.com/resources/scripture-engagement/one-another/

- **Sir Isaac Newton's Religious Writings:**
  http://www.newtonproject.ox.ac.uk/

- **Word Study: Mandatum (Commandment):**
  https://biblehub.com/greek/1785.htm

Reflection

Take a few minutes to reflect and meditate on what you just read. Write down your thoughts take time to pray and praise God.

_____

_____

_____

_____

_____

_____

_____

_____

_____

_____

_____

_____

_____

_____

_____

_____

_____

Day 23

Choose

If it is disagreeable in your sight to serve the Lord, choose for yourselves today whom you will serve: whether the gods which your fathers served which were beyond the River, or the gods of the Amorites in whose land you are living; but as for me and my house, we will serve the Lord."
Joshua 24:15

For this chapter, we are moving to the dusty plains of Shechem, where an old warrior is giving his final "locker room" speech. It's a moment of high drama and ultimate decision.

Chapter 23: The Line in the Sand

Key Verse: *"If it is disagreeable in your sight to serve the Lord, choose for yourselves today whom you will serve... but as for me and my house, we will serve the Lord." —* **Joshua 24:15 (NASB)**

The Myth of the Middle Ground

Have you ever tried to stand with one foot in a boat and one foot on the dock? It works for a second or two, but as soon as the water ripples, you find yourself in a very uncomfortable — and wet — situation. You eventually have to pick a side.

Life is full of choices. We choose what to wear, what to eat, and which path to take to work. But Joshua, the man who led Israel into the Promised Land, points out that there is one choice that stands above all others. It is the choice of **mastery**. He tells the people that they cannot just "drift" through life. They have to intentionally **choose** who they are going to serve.

The world likes to tell us that we can stay in the "middle ground." We think we can be "spiritual" without being committed, or that we can follow God when it's convenient and follow our own desires when it's not. But Joshua draws a line in the sand. He says that even "no choice" is actually a choice to serve the culture around you.

What Does it Mean to Choose?

The word "choose" in this passage (*bachar*) means to examine carefully and then select. It isn't a "gut feeling" or a lucky guess. It's a decision made with your eyes wide open.

Joshua was an old man when he said this. He had seen God part the Jordan River, and he had seen the walls of Jericho fall. But he had also seen the people grumble and turn back to old habits. He knew that yesterday's choice wasn't enough for today. Every sun that rises brings a new requirement to pick our side of the line.

A Lesson from History: Patrick Henry's Choice

In the history of the United States, there is perhaps no more famous moment of "choosing" than Patrick Henry's speech in 1775. The colonies were at a crossroads. They could continue to serve the British Crown, which many felt had become a "master" that didn't care for them, or they could choose the dangerous path of liberty.

Henry didn't believe in the middle ground. He saw that the time for "drifting" was over. He famously ended his speech with words that echoed Joshua's "as for me" resolve:

"I know not what course others may take; but as for me, give me liberty or give me death!"

Henry understood that some things are worth everything. For Joshua, the choice wasn't about political liberty, but about spiritual life. He was saying, "I don't care what the rest of the world does. My house has already made its decision."

The Gods of the "Beyond"

Joshua tells the people they can choose the gods their fathers served "beyond the River" or the gods of the land where they were currently living.

Today, our "gods" look a little different, but they are just as demanding.

- **The God of Comfort:** Choosing to do what is easy rather than what is right.

- **The God of Approval:** Choosing to act in a way that makes people like us, even if it ignores God's commands.

- **The God of Self:** Choosing to be the king or queen of our own little universe.

When we don't actively choose the Lord, we default to serving these "gods." They promise happiness, but they always leave us empty. Joshua knew that only the Lord — the God who actually kept His promises — was worthy of the "All-In" choice.

The Story of the Two Anchors

Imagine a ship caught in a massive storm. The captain has two anchors. One is made of heavy iron, and the other is a beautiful, gold-painted plastic prop left over from a movie set.

If the captain doesn't **choose** to drop the iron anchor, the ship will be driven onto the rocks. The "plastic" anchor might look nicer, and it might be easier to handle, but it has no power to hold the ship.

Choosing to serve the Lord is dropping the iron anchor. It might be heavy, and it might require some work to "set," but it is the only thing that will keep your life from being smashed when the "storms" of life arrive.

Wisdom from a "Man of Integrity"

John Adams, the second President of the United States, was a man who believed that a nation could only survive if its people chose to live by a high moral code. He knew that the choices made in private determined the strength of a person in public.

Adams once wrote:

"Duty is ours; events are God's."

This is the essence of Joshua's choice. Our job is to choose the "duty" of serving God today. We don't have to worry about the "events" or how things turn out (remember "Casting your burden" from Chapter 21?). Our only responsibility is the choice of who is in charge of our hearts.

How to "Choose" Today

Choosing to serve the Lord isn't just something you did years ago at a church altar. It's something you do at 7:00 AM on a Monday.

1. **The "Morning Declaration":** Before you even get out of bed, say it out loud: "As for me and my house, we will serve the Lord today." This sets the "tone" for your brain (Chapter 5).

2. **The "Fork in the Road" Pause:** When you face a decision today — even a small one like how to respond to an annoying email — pause and ask: "Which choice serves my new Master, and which choice serves my old self?"

3. **The Household Huddle:** If you live with others, talk about what it looks like for your "house" to serve God. Maybe it means being the most hospitable house on the block, or the one that is known for never gossiping.

The great theologian and educator Jonathan Edwards once made a series of "Resolutions" for his life. His first one was:

"Resolved, that I will do whatsoever I think to be most to God's glory... whether now, or never so many myriads of ages hence."

Edwards chose his "side" and never looked back.

A Moment for Reflection

Whose "uniform" are you wearing today? (Remember Chapter 22). If a stranger watched your life for 24 hours, would they be able to tell who you serve?

Don't let your life be something that just "happens" to you. Don't let the culture mold you into its shape (Chapter 8). Stand up, look at the line in the sand, and make the choice. You don't have to wait for the rest of the world to join you. Even if you are the only one in your office, your neighborhood, or your social circle, you can say, "As for me... I've made my choice."

Closing Prayer

Lord, I thank You that You chose me before I ever chose You. I confess that I've spent too much time trying to keep one foot in the world and one foot in Your kingdom. Today, I'm making my choice. I choose to serve You with my time, my money, and my heart. Let my life be a clear sign to everyone around me that I belong to You. Amen.

References and Further Reading

- **The Life and Resolutions of Jonathan Edwards:**
  https://www.christianitytoday.com/history/people/theologians/jonathan-edwards.html

- **Patrick Henry's "Liberty or Death" Speech:**
  https://www.history.com/topics/american-revolution/patrick-henry

- **John Adams on Duty and Providence:**
  https://www.masshist.org/digitaladams/archive/

- **Word Study: Bachar (Choose):**
  https://biblehub.com/hebrew/977.htm

Reflection

Take a few minutes to reflect and meditate on what you just read. Write down your thoughts take time to pray and praise God.

_____

_____

_____

_____

_____

_____

_____

_____

_____

_____

_____

_____

_____

_____

_____

_____

_____

_____

Day 24

Continue

So Jesus was saying to those Jews who had believed Him, "If you continue in My word, then you are truly disciples of Mine; and you will know the truth, and the truth will make you free."
John 8:31-32

The purpose of this chapter is to shift our understanding of faith from a **momentary decision** to a **continual dwelling**. While many "believe," Jesus calls us to "abide"—to move from being occasional visitors of the Word to permanent residents.

By exploring the Greek concept of *meno* (continuity), the persistent legacy of William Tyndale, and the metaphor of the spiritual anchor, this chapter demonstrates that true freedom is found not in our own impulses, but in the steady, daily pursuit of Truth. You will learn how to combat "spiritual drift" and establish a lifestyle of consistency that sustains you through every season of life.

Chapter 24: The Freedom of the Constant

Key Verse: *"So Jesus was saying to those Jews who had believed Him, 'If you continue in My word, then you are truly disciples of Mine; and you will know the truth, and the truth will make you free.'"* — **John 8:31-32 (NASB)**

The Condition of Continuity

In a world characterized by short attention spans and fleeting interests, Jesus introduces a radical concept for spiritual growth: **Continuity.**

The setting for this verse is crucial. Jesus is speaking to a crowd of people who "believed" Him. On the surface, they had made a start. But Jesus clarifies that belief is not just a point in time; it is a posture for a lifetime. He uses the word **"continue"** (the Greek word *meno*), which means to abide, remain, or dwell.

True discipleship is not defined by the initial excitement of a new idea, but by the "remaining" in that truth when the novelty wears off.

In the ancient world, a disciple was more than a student; they were an apprentice who lived so closely with their master that they began to think, talk, and act exactly like them. You cannot apprentice yourself to someone you only visit occasionally.

The Truth That Frees

Jesus links our "continuing" to two specific results:

1. **Knowledge:** You will *know* the truth.

2. **Freedom:** The truth will *make you free.*

The "freedom" Jesus speaks of is not the freedom to do whatever we want; it is the freedom to be who we were created to be. Without the "North Star" of God's Word (Chapter 9), we are slaves to our impulses, the opinions of others, and the "mold" of the world (Chapter 8). When we abide in the Word, we are set free from the lies that tell us we aren't enough or that our value is found in "earthly things."

A Lesson from History: William Tyndale's Persistence

To understand what it means to "continue in the Word," we look back at William Tyndale. As we discussed earlier Tyndale was committed to getting the Bible into the hands of the common man.

But what stands out about Tyndale was his **continuity**. He was forced to flee England and lived as a fugitive for years in Europe. He faced poverty, betrayal, and the constant threat of arrest. Despite this, he "continued." He spent his days and nights translating, revising, and printing.

He didn't just "start" the translation; he remained in the Word until the work was finished. Because he continued, millions of people were eventually able to "know the truth" in their own language. Tyndale understood that the Word was a "living thing" that had to be inhabited, not just read.

The Anchor of the Soul

The concept of *meno* (abiding) is like an anchor.

Imagine a boat on the ocean. If the boat is not anchored, the current will slowly carry it away from the shore. The change is so gradual that the people on the boat might not even notice until they are miles out at sea. This is "spiritual drift."

By "continuing" in the Word—through daily reading, meditation, and prayer—we drop an anchor. The currents of culture and the winds of hardship will still blow, but because we are "anchored" in the Word, we stay where we belong.

Wisdom from the "Prince of Preachers"

Charles Spurgeon, whom we've referenced regarding mental discipline, was a staunch advocate for the "continuing" life. He famously said:

"Visit many books, but live in the Bible."

Spurgeon believed that while other knowledge was useful, only the Word of God provided the "freedom" Jesus promised. He taught that the Bible should be the "house" we live in, not just a place we visit when we are in trouble.

How to "Continue" Today

Continuity is a discipline that fights against the "noise" of modern life. Here is how you can practice John 8:31-32 today:

1. **The "Abide" Morning:** Before checking emails or news, spend five minutes "remaining" in a single passage of Scripture. Read it slowly three times. Let it sink in.

2. **The "Truth Filter":** When you hear a negative thought ("I'm not good enough," "This situation is hopeless"), ask: "Does this line up with what I know from the Word?" If not, reject the lie and replace it with the truth.

3. **The "Long Walk" Mentality:** Remind yourself that spiritual maturity is a slow process. Don't get discouraged if you don't feel "different" after one day. Continuity is about the direction of your life, not the speed of your progress.

As the great philosopher and scientist Blaise Pascal noted:

"Truth is so obscure in these times, and falsehood so established, that, unless we love the truth, we cannot know it."

To "continue" is to show that you love the truth enough to stay with it.

A Moment for Reflection

Are you a "visitor" to the Word or a "resident"? Do you turn to God's truth only when you are in a crisis, or is it the atmosphere you breathe every day?

Jesus isn't looking for a crowd of "believers" who cheer for Him today and forget Him tomorrow. He is looking for disciples who will walk with Him through the dust, the hills, and the valleys. Today, make the decision to stay. Don't just read the Word; live in it.

Closing Prayer

Lord, I thank You for the truth that sets me free. I confess that I often drift away from Your Word when life gets busy or distracting. Please help me to "abide" in You today. Give me a hunger for Your truth and the persistence to continue even when I don't feel like it. May Your Word be the home where my heart always returns. Amen.

References and Further Reading

- **The Theology of "Abiding" (Meno):**
  https://www.blueletterbible.org/lexicon/g3306/nasb95/mgnt/0-1/

- **William Tyndale's Life of Persistence:**
  https://www.christianitytoday.com/history/people/scholarsandscientists/william-tyndale.html

- **Spurgeon's "All of Grace" on Consistency:**
  https://www.spurgeon.org/resource-library/books/all-of-grace/

- **Pascal on Truth and Falsehood:**
  https://www.gutenberg.org/files/2412/2412-h/2412-h.htm

Reflection

Take a few minutes to reflect and meditate on what you just read.   Write down your thoughts take time to pray and praise God.

_____

_____

_____

_____

_____

_____

_____

_____

_____

_____

_____

_____

_____

_____

_____

_____

_____

Day 25

Render

And Jesus said to them, "Render to Caesar the things that are Caesar's, and to God the things that are God's." And they were amazed at Him.
Mark 12:17

This chapter addresses one of the most famous confrontations in the New Testament. It moves us from the internal discipline of "continuing" in the Word to the external reality of living as a citizen of two different worlds. Jesus provides a profound principle that defines our obligations to both human authority and Divine sovereignty.

Chapter 25: The Dual Citizenship

Key Verse: *"And Jesus said to them, 'Render to Caesar the things that are Caesar's, and to God the things that are God's.' And they were amazed at Him."*
— **Mark 12:17 (NASB)**

The Trap of the Coin

To understand the weight of the word **"render,"** we have to look at the trap being set for Jesus. The religious leaders brought Him a political landmine: "Is it lawful to pay a poll-tax to Caesar, or not?"

If Jesus said "Yes," the Jewish people would view Him as a traitor to Israel. If He said "No," the Roman authorities would arrest Him for sedition. It seemed like an impossible choice. But Jesus asked for a denarius—a common Roman coin—and asked whose likeness was on it. When they said "Caesar's," He gave a command that bypassed their trap and established a timeless truth.

The word "render" in Greek is *apodidomi*. It is stronger than the word for "give." It means to "pay back" or to "return what is owed." Jesus was saying that if Caesar's face is on the metal, he has a legitimate claim to that metal. Pay your taxes. Follow the laws. But then He added the second half, which changed the world.

The Divine Image

If the coin belongs to Caesar because it bears his image, then what belongs to God? The answer is found in the very first chapter of the Bible: **You.**

Genesis 1:27 tells us that human beings are created in the **image of God**. Just as Caesar's likeness was stamped into the silver, God's likeness is stamped into your very soul. We "render" taxes to the government because we live in their territory, but we "render" our worship, our character, and our ultimate allegiance to God because we belong to His Kingdom.

A Lesson from History: Sir Thomas More

One of the most powerful historical examples of "rendering" to both spheres is Sir Thomas More, the 16th-century Lord Chancellor of England. More was a loyal servant to King Henry VIII. He worked tirelessly for the state and was a brilliant lawyer and diplomat. He "rendered to Caesar" his hard work and his legal expertise for decades.

However, when King Henry VIII demanded that More sign an oath declaring the King to be the Supreme Head of the Church of England, More reached a limit. He could not render to the King the authority that he believed belonged only to God.

More was imprisoned and eventually executed. His final words on the scaffold perfectly captured the balance of Mark 12:17:

"I die the King's good servant, but God's first."

He understood that while he owed the King his service, he owed God his conscience.

The Conflict of Allegiance

Most of the time, our duties to the state and to God do not conflict. We are commanded to be the best citizens, the most honest taxpayers, and the most helpful neighbors. By being "good servants" of the community, we often reflect the glory of the Father.

However, the "Render" principle reminds us that our primary identity is not found in our political party, our nationality, or our social status. Those are all "coins" that belong to this temporary world. Our primary identity is found in the "likeness" we carry—the image of the Creator.

Wisdom from the "Father of the Constitution"

James Madison, a primary architect of the American system of government, thought deeply about the "Render" principle. He believed that the state has no right to claim the "things that are God's," specifically a person's religious convictions.

Madison wrote:

"The Religion then of every man must be left to the conviction and conscience of every man; and it is the right of every man to exercise it as these may dictate."

Madison recognized that for a society to function, there had to be a clear distinction between what a citizen owes to the government (taxes, following laws) and what a soul owes to the Creator (faith and worship).

How to "Render" Correctly Today

Living as a "dual citizen" requires daily discernment. Here is how to apply Mark 12:17 this week:

1. **The "Image" Audit:** When you look in the mirror, remind yourself: "I am God's property. I bear His image." Let that truth dictate how you treat your body and your mind today.

2. **Honest Citizenship:** Render to "Caesar" (your boss, your government, your school) excellence and honesty. Don't cut corners on your taxes or your work hours. A Christian should be the most reliable person in any organization.

3. **The Priority Check:** If you find yourself more distressed by political news than by your own spiritual growth, you might be

giving too much of your heart to "Caesar." Re-center your focus on "the things that are God's."

As the great 19th-century theologian Abraham Kuyper famously said:

"There is not a square inch in the whole domain of our human existence over which Christ, who is Sovereign over all, does not cry: 'Mine!'"

A Moment for Reflection

Are you trying to give God "Caesar's coins" while keeping "God's image" for yourself? We often try to buy God off with a little bit of money or a few hours of service, while we keep our hearts and our deepest desires for ourselves.

Jesus isn't interested in your coins; He is interested in the "metal" that bears His likeness. Today, give the world what it is owed, but make sure you haven't held back the one thing that belongs to God — your whole self.

Closing Prayer

Lord, I thank You that You have stamped Your image upon my soul. Help me to be a person of integrity who fulfills my duties to the world around me. Give me the wisdom to know the difference between what belongs to the state and what belongs only to You. I render my life, my will, and my worship to You today. Amen.

References and Further Reading

- **The Life and Trial of Sir Thomas More:**
  https://www.britannica.com/biography/Thomas-More

- **James Madison on Religious Freedom:**
  https://www.archives.gov/founding-docs/memorial-and-remonstrance

- **Abraham Kuyper's "Sphere Sovereignty":**
  https://www.acton.org/pub/religion-liberty/volume-6-number-5/sphere-sovereignty

- **Word Study: Apodidomi (Render):**
  https://biblehub.com/greek/591.htm

. **Reflection**

Take a few minutes to reflect and meditate on what you just read. Write down your thoughts take time to pray and praise God.

_____

_____

_____

_____

_____

_____

_____

_____

_____

_____

_____

_____

_____

_____

_____

_____

Day 26

Watch & Pray

In the morning, O Lord, You will hear my voice; In the morning I will order my prayer to You and eagerly watch.
Psalm 5:3

Keep watching and praying that you may not enter into temptation; the spirit is willing, but the flesh is weak."
Matthew 26:41

This chapter addresses the vital connection between our spiritual alertness and our active communication with God. While many people treat prayer as a last resort or a late-night afterthought, the Bible presents it as a morning priority and a continuous defensive strategy. We move now into the discipline of spiritual vigilance.

Chapter 26: The Morning Watch

Key Verses: *"In the morning, O Lord, You will hear my voice; in the morning I will order my prayer to You and eagerly watch."* — **Psalm 5:3 (NASB)**

"Keep watching and praying that you may not come into temptation; the spirit is willing, but the flesh is weak." — **Matthew 26:41 (NASB)**

The Order of the Day

The Hebrew word used by David in Psalm 5:3 for "order" (*arak*) is a fascinating technical term. It was used to describe the way a priest would "arrange" the wood upon the altar for a sacrifice or how a general would "set in array" his troops for battle.

David didn't just "say a prayer"; he **ordered** his prayer. He laid it out with purpose. But notice what he does after he finishes praying: he **eagerly watches**. Most of us pray and then go about our day, forgetting what we even asked for. David prayed and then stood on his "watchtower," waiting to see how God would move.

The Willing Spirit and the Weak Flesh

Fast forward to the Garden of Gethsemane in Matthew 26. Jesus is facing the greatest "battle" of His life, and He asks His disciples to do one thing: **Watch and pray.** He highlights the fundamental struggle of the human condition: "the spirit is willing, but the flesh is weak."

We often have the *intention* to be strong, to be patient, or to be faithful, but our "flesh"—our natural, human weakness—betrays us when the pressure is on.

Jesus reveals the secret to overcoming this weakness. It isn't just "trying harder." It is the combination of **watching** (staying alert to the reality of spiritual battle) and **praying** (connecting to the source of Divine strength). If you watch without praying, you will be overwhelmed by what you see. If you pray without watching, you will be blindsided by the "temptation" you didn't see coming.

A Lesson from History: The "Iron Duke" at Waterloo

The Duke of Wellington, the man who defeated Napoleon at the Battle of Waterloo, was a master of "watching and praying" in a military sense. He was known for his extreme vigilance. He would often spend the night before a battle personally scouting the terrain, "watching" for any advantage or hidden danger.

But Wellington was also a man of faith. He understood that his own "flesh" and military genius were not enough. He famously remarked:

"The only thing I am afraid of is fear."

He knew that if his spirit faltered, the battle was lost. He maintained a discipline of order and prayer, recognizing that victory was ultimately in the hands of Providence. Like David, he "ordered" his forces and then "watched" with intense focus for the moment to strike.

The Sentinel's Post

In the ancient world, a sentinel (a watchman) had one job: to stay awake when everyone else was sleeping. If the watchman fell asleep, the city was defenseless.

Temptation often arrives like a thief in the night. It rarely walks through the front door with a loud announcement. It creeps in through a small compromise, a moment of bitterness, or a wandering thought (Chapter 5). By "watching and praying," we are putting a guard at the door of our hearts. We are identifying the "weak spots" in our walls before the enemy can exploit them.

Wisdom from the "Prince of Preachers"

Charles Spurgeon, whom we have visited throughout this study, compared prayer to the breath of the soul. He taught that "watching" was the eyes of the soul and "praying" was the voice.

Spurgeon said:

"Prayer is the rope in the belfry; it pulls the bell in heaven."

But he warned that we must not just pull the rope and walk away; we must stay and listen for the "bell" to ring. This is the "eagerly watching" that David describes. It is the expectation that God is actually listening and will actually respond.

How to "Watch and Pray" Today

This is a proactive discipline that changes the way you face your day.

1. **The Orderly Morning:** Don't let your first act of the day be checking your phone. "Order" your prayer. List your concerns, your family, and your "weaknesses" before the Lord.

2. **The "Check-Post" Moments:** Throughout the day, set a "watch." When you feel a surge of anger or a temptation to be dishonest, pause and pray immediately. This is "watching" for the trap before you step in it.

3. **Expectant Watching:** After you pray for something, look for the answer. Keep a "prayer journal" where you can record how God "ordered" the events of your day in response to your morning watch.

By making "watch and pray" a daily habit, you are weaving a cable of spiritual strength that the "weakness of the flesh" cannot snap.

A Moment for Reflection

Are you spiritually "asleep at the wheel"? Do you find yourself constantly surprised by your own failures or overwhelmed by your circumstances?

Jesus' command in the Garden wasn't just for the twelve disciples; it was for you. He knows your spirit is willing. He knows you want to finish well. But He also knows your flesh is weak. Today, don't just rely on your intentions. Order your prayer, take your post on the watchtower, and look toward the horizon. The King is listening, and the Morning Star is rising.

Closing Prayer

Lord, I thank You that You never sleep or slumber. I confess that I often fall asleep on my watch. I rely on my own strength and forget how weak my flesh really is. Today, I order my prayer to You and I choose to eagerly watch for Your hand at work. Give me the alertness to see temptation before it strikes and the faith to pray through every battle. Amen.

References and Further Reading

- **Word Study: Arak (Order) and Tsaphah (Watch):**
  https://www.blueletterbible.org/lexicon/h6635/nasb95/wlc/0-1/

- **The Duke of Wellington's Faith and Discipline:**
  https://www.historytoday.com/archive/wellington-and-waterloo

- **Spurgeon on the "Watchman's Cry":**
  https://www.spurgeon.org/resource-library/sermons/the-watchmans-cry/

- **The Psychology of Habit (Horace Mann):**
  https://www.britannica.com/biography/Horace-Mann

Reflection

Take a few minutes to reflect and meditate on what you just read. Write down your thoughts take time to pray and praise God.

_____

_____

_____

_____

_____

_____

_____

_____

_____

_____

_____

_____

_____

_____

_____

_____

Day 27

Repent

From that time Jesus began to preach and say, "Repent, for the kingdom of heaven is at hand."
Matthew 4:17

This chapter addresses the very first word of Jesus' public ministry. It is a word that is often misunderstood as merely a threat or a religious formality, but in reality, it is an invitation to a total transformation of life. As we move toward finishing well, we must understand that we cannot move forward in a new direction until we have officially turned away from the old one.

Chapter 27: The Great About-Face

Key Verse: *"From that time Jesus began to preach and say, 'Repent, for the kingdom of heaven is at hand.'"* — **Matthew 4:17 (NASB)**

The U-Turn of the Soul

The word "repent" has been hijacked by pop culture to mean someone shouting on a street corner. But the biblical meaning is far more profound. In the original Greek, the word is *metanoia*. It is a compound word: *meta* (change) and *noia* (mind). It literally means **a change of mind that leads to a change of direction.**

Imagine you are driving down a highway, convinced you are heading toward your destination. Suddenly, you see a sign that proves you are driving 180 degrees in the wrong direction. "Repentance" is the moment you realize the error, exit the highway, and make a U-turn. It isn't just feeling bad about being lost; it is the physical act of turning the car around.

Jesus wasn't just asking people to feel sorry for their sins. He was telling them that a new Kingdom had arrived, and their old way of thinking and living wouldn't work in this new reality. To enter the Kingdom of Heaven, they had to change their mental GPS.

A Lesson from History: The "Amazing Grace" of John Newton

Perhaps the most famous story of *metanoia* in history is that of John Newton. In the mid-1700s, Newton was a slave trader. He was a man who lived a life of profanity, violence, and the literal enslavement of other human beings. He was heading at full speed in the "wrong direction."

During a violent storm at sea in 1748, Newton cried out to God for mercy. That moment was the beginning of his repentance. He didn't just "feel guilty"; he eventually left the slave trade entirely, became a minister, and worked alongside William Wilberforce to abolish slavery in England.

Newton's change of mind led to a total change of life. He captured this "U-turn" in the lyrics of his famous hymn:

"I once was lost, but now am found; was blind, but now I see."

Newton understood that repentance isn't a one-time emotional event; it is a permanent change in how you see the world and your place in it.

The Kingdom is "At Hand"

Why does Jesus say we should repent? **"For the kingdom of heaven is at hand."** This means the Kingdom is within reach; it is right here. We often think of repentance as a way to avoid punishment, but Jesus presents it as a way to access a better life. It's like a person holding a handful of pebbles who is offered a handful of diamonds. They have to "repent" (change their mind) about the value of the pebbles and drop them before they can receive the diamonds.

If we want to finish well, we have to identify the "pebbles" we are clinging to—our pride, our secret habits, our need for control—and drop them so we can grasp the "diamonds" of the Kingdom: peace, joy, and eternal purpose.

The Counterfeit of Repentance

It is important to distinguish between true repentance and **remorse**.

- **Remorse** is Judas Iscariot. He felt terrible about what he did, but he didn't turn back to God. He stayed trapped in his guilt.

- **Repentance** is the Apostle Peter. After denying Jesus three times, he wept bitterly, but then he turned back. He allowed his failure to change his heart, and he became the leader of the early church.

Remorse looks at the sin; Repentance looks at the Savior. Remorse leads to despair; Repentance leads to "times of refreshing" (**Acts 3:19**).

Wisdom from the "Prince of Preachers"

Charles Spurgeon described repentance as a "holy arrow" that must be shot from the bow of the heart.

He once said:

"Repentance is a discovery of the evil of sin, a mourning that we have ever committed it, a resolution to forsake it. It is, in fact, a change of mind of a very deep and practical character."

Spurgeon emphasized that you cannot claim to have repented of a sin that you are still intentionally practicing. True *metanoia* always shows up in the "Next Steps" of our behavior.

How to Practice Repentance Today

Repentance is a daily "re-alignment" of the soul. Here is how you can apply Matthew 4:17 today:

1. **The Honest Inventory:** Ask God to show you one area where you are "blind"—a habit or attitude that is heading in the wrong direction. Don't make excuses; just acknowledge it.

2. **The 180-Degree Action:** If you have been "moving toward" bitterness, make a deliberate turn toward forgiveness. If you have been "moving toward" greed, make a deliberate turn toward giving (Chapter 11).

3. **Celebrate the Kingdom:** Remember that you aren't turning *away* from fun; you are turning *toward* the Kingdom of Heaven. Every time you repent, you are stepping into a higher, better way of living.

Repentance is the "thriftiness" of the soul. It is refusing to waste another minute heading in the wrong direction.

A Moment for Reflection

Is there a "signpost" in your life right now telling you that you're on the wrong road? Perhaps it's a nagging conscience, a broken relationship, or a sense of spiritual emptiness.

Don't ignore the sign. Repentance isn't a dirty word; it is the most beautiful word in the language of grace. It means you don't have to keep going where you're going. You can stop. You can turn. You can come home. The Kingdom is at hand, and the Father is waiting at the U-turn with open arms.

Closing Prayer

Lord, I thank You that You don't leave me lost in my own wrong directions. I confess that I often try to justify my paths instead of repenting. Today, I choose to change my mind. Show me where I am blind, and give me the courage to make a total U-turn toward Your Kingdom. I drop my pebbles to reach for Your diamonds. Amen.

References and Further Reading

- **The Life and Conversion of John Newton:**
  https://www.christianitytoday.com/history/people/poets/john-newton.html

- **Word Study: Metanoia (Repentance):**
  https://biblehub.com/greek/3341.htm

- **Spurgeon on "The Great Turn":**
  https://www.spurgeon.org/resource-library/sermons/repentance-unto-life/

Reflection

Take a few minutes to reflect and meditate on what you just read. Write down your thoughts take time to pray and praise God.

_____

_____

_____

_____

_____

_____

_____

_____

_____

_____

_____

_____

_____

_____

_____

_____

Day 28

Love Your Enemies

But I say to you, love your enemies and pray for those who persecute you,
Matthew 5:44

This chapter confronts what is arguably the most difficult command in the entire Bible. We have discussed loving "one another", but Jesus now takes the principle of love and pushes it into the territory of the impossible. To finish well, we must learn to handle the people who actively work against us.

Chapter 28: The Impossible Love

Key Verse: *"But I say to you, love your enemies and pray for those who persecute you."* — **Matthew 5:44 (NASB)**

The Radical Shift

In the natural world, there is a law of reciprocity: you get what you give. If someone is kind to you, you are kind back. If someone strikes you, the natural "flesh" wants to strike back. Even the ancient religious laws had established a limit on retaliation: "an eye for an eye."

But Jesus steps onto the scene and shatters the law of reciprocity. He introduces a supernatural standard. The word for "love" here is *agape* — a love of the will, not of the emotions. It is a decision to seek the highest good of another person, regardless of how they treat you.

Jesus isn't asking you to have "warm feelings" for your enemy. He is commanding you to act in their best interest and to bring their names before God in prayer.

A Lesson from History: Abraham Lincoln's "Destroyed" Enemies

Abraham Lincoln, whom we have looked to for his humility and trust, lived out Matthew 5:44 during the most bitter conflict in American history. He was constantly attacked, not just by the South, but by his own cabinet and the Northern press. One of his fiercest critics was Edwin Stanton, who called Lincoln a "low, cunning clown" and an "original gorilla."

How did Lincoln respond? He didn't retaliate. He didn't "flee". Instead, recognizing Stanton's brilliance, he appointed him Secretary of War. Lincoln treated his enemy with respect and sought the best for the country through him.

When Lincoln was assassinated, it was Stanton who stood by his bed and famously said through tears, "Now he belongs to the ages." Lincoln had followed his own famous proverb:

"Am I not destroying my enemies when I make friends of them?"

The Purpose of the Persecutor

Why would God command us to love people who want to hurt us?

1. **To Mirror the Father:** Jesus explains in the following verses that God sends rain on the just and the unjust. When we love our enemies, we prove we are "sons of our Father."

2. **To Break the Chain:** Hate is a chain reaction. It only stops when it hits someone who refuses to pass it on.

3. **To Transform the Self:** Loving an enemy requires a level of spiritual strength that nothing else can produce. It forces you to rely entirely on the Holy Spirit because your "flesh" simply cannot do it.

The Story of the Forgiving Guard

During the mid-20th century, many Christians were imprisoned for their faith in various parts of the world. One story tells of a prisoner who was consistently beaten by a specific guard. Instead of cursing the guard, the prisoner began to pray for him every day.

One day, the guard asked, "Why don't you hate me? I have taken everything from you." The prisoner replied, "You have taken my freedom, but you cannot take my love, because it isn't mine—it's Christ's love in me." The guard was so shaken by this "impossible love" that he eventually sought the truth for himself. The "light" of the prisoner (Chapter 13) was brightest when the darkness was most intense.

Wisdom from the "Prince of Preachers"

Charles Spurgeon taught that the way we treat our enemies is the ultimate "litmus test" of our faith.

He once said:

"If you cannot forgive, you can have no claim to be forgiven. If you cannot love those who hate you, you have not the spirit of Christ."

Spurgeon noted that it is easy to love those who love us—even "tax collectors" do that. The mark of the Christian is the ability to do what is unnatural.

How to Love Your Enemies Today

This is a high-level spiritual discipline. Here is how you can apply Matthew 5:44 this week:

1. **The Prayer List:** Identify the person who "persecutes" you. It might be a difficult boss, a family member who mocks your faith, or someone who gossiped about you. Put their name on your prayer list.

2. **Blessing with the Tongue:** When their name comes up in conversation, refuse to say anything negative. Find one true, positive thing to say, or stay silent. This is "rendering" good for evil (Chapter 18).

3. **The Small Act of Good:** If you find an opportunity to do a small favor for this person — without them necessarily knowing it was you — do it.

When we pray for our enemies, we are bringing the any "hidden" conflict into the light of God's presence, where fear and bitterness lose their power.

A Moment for Reflection

Is there a "debt" you are trying to collect from someone who hurt you? Are you waiting for an apology that may never come?

By refusing to love and forgive, you are staying tethered to your enemy. You are allowing them to dictate your emotional state. When you "agape" love them and pray for them, you are cutting the rope. You are letting God handle the justice (Chapter 1) while you focus on the "good works" (Chapter 13). Today, release the debt. Pray for the person who hurt you. Step into the supernatural freedom of the "impossible love."

Closing Prayer

Lord, I confess that I do not want to love my enemies. My flesh wants justice and retaliation. But I thank You that You loved me while I was Your enemy. Please pour Your supernatural love into my heart. Give me the strength to pray for those who hurt me and the grace to seek their good. May my life reflect Your mercy to a world that only knows how to hate. Amen.

References and Further Reading

- **Lincoln and Stanton: A Study in Forgiveness:** https://www.nps.gov/vick/learn/historyculture/edwin-m-stanton.htm

- **Word Study: Agape (Love):** https://biblehub.com/greek/26.htm

- **Spurgeon's "Love Your Enemies" Sermon:** https://www.spurgeon.org/resource-library/sermons/love-your-enemies/

Reflection

Take a few minutes to reflect and meditate on what you just read. Write down your thoughts take time to pray and praise God.

_____

_____

_____

_____

_____

_____

_____

_____

_____

_____

_____

_____

_____

_____

_____

_____

Day 29

Be Reconciled

Therefore if you are presenting your offering at the altar, and there remember that your brother has something against you, leave your offering there before the altar and go; first be reconciled to your brother, and then come and present your offering.
Matthew 5:23-24

This chapter addresses the urgent necessity of horizontal restoration. We have just explored the "impossible love" required for enemies (Day 28), and now Jesus narrows the focus to those within our immediate circles. He presents a teaching so radical that it places the act of reconciliation above the act of formal worship.

Chapter 29: The Priority of Peace

Key Verse: *"Therefore if you are presenting your offering at the altar, and there remember that your brother has something against you, leave your offering there before the altar and go; first be reconciled to your brother, and then come and present your offering."* — **Matthew 5:23-24 (NASB)**

The Interrupted Sacrifice

In the Jewish tradition of Jesus' day, the walk to the Temple to present an offering was the highest religious duty a person could perform. It was a journey of devotion, often involving travel, expense, and careful preparation. Yet, Jesus describes a scene where this "holy" moment is suddenly interrupted by a memory: "your brother has something against you."

Notice that Jesus does not say, "if *you* have something against your brother." That would be about your own forgiveness. Instead, He says if someone else has a grievance against *you*. Jesus commands the worshiper to stop mid-ceremony, leave the gift at the altar, and go.

The word **"reconciled"** in Greek is *diallasso*. It means to change thoroughly — to move from a state of enmity to a state of friendship. Jesus is teaching that God is more interested in the state of your relationships than the ceremony of your religion.

A Lesson from History: The Reconciliation of the "Founding Brothers"

One of the most moving examples of *diallasso* in history is the reconciliation between John Adams and Thomas Jefferson. These two men were once close friends, but they became bitter political rivals. For over a decade, they lived in a state of icy silence, each harboring grievances against the other.

It was Benjamin Rush, a fellow signer of the Declaration of Independence, who acted as a "peacemaker." He encouraged them to reach out. In 1812, Adams finally "left his offering" and sent a brief, friendly note to Jefferson. This sparked a series of letters that lasted the rest of their lives.

They chose to be reconciled before it was too late. They both died on the same day — July 4, 1826 — at peace with one another. Adams understood that the legacy of their "house" (Chapter 16) depended on their ability to settle their differences. As Jefferson later wrote:

"I find friendship to be the wine of life."

The "First" Principle

Jesus uses the word **"first."** *"First be reconciled... and then come."* This is a matter of priority. We often try to use our "vertical" relationship with God to hide the "horizontal" wreckage of our relationships with people.

We think that if we pray enough, or give enough, God will overlook our bitterness or our refusal to make things right.

But the Bible is clear: you cannot be right with the Father while you are intentionally wrong with His other children. Your "offering"—whether it is your time, your money, or your service—is tainted if it is being used as a substitute for an apology or a restitution.

The Story of the Half-Built Bridge

Imagine a man who decides to build a bridge across a wide chasm to reach a beautiful temple. He spends years building the bridge from his side, using the finest stone and the most beautiful carvings. But when he gets halfway across, he stops. He refuses to connect the bridge to the other side because he dislikes the person who lives there.

No matter how beautiful his half of the bridge is, it is useless. He can never reach the temple because the bridge isn't finished. Our relationships are the "other half" of our bridge to God. If we refuse to connect with our brother, our path to the "Altar" remains incomplete.

Wisdom from the "Prince of Preachers"

Charles Spurgeon warned that an unforgiving or unreconciled heart acts as a "dam" that blocks the flow of God's grace.

He once remarked:

"He who will not forgive his brother has not felt the power of the blood of Christ in his own soul... Reconciliation to God is always accompanied by reconciliation to men."

Spurgeon emphasized that "going" to the brother is an act of humility. It requires us to lay down our "right" to be right for the sake of the peace of the Kingdom.

How to "Be Reconciled" Today

Reconciliation is an active verb. It requires movement. Here is how you can apply Matthew 5:23-24 this week:

1. **The Altar Memory:** The next time you sit down to pray or enter a church service, ask the Holy Spirit: "Is there anyone who has something against me?" Listen to the names that come to mind.

2. **The "Go" Initiative:** Don't wait for them to come to you. Even if they are 90% at fault, take responsibility for your 10%. Make the phone call, send the text, or request the meeting.

3. **The Simple Apology:** True reconciliation doesn't require a complex debate. It often starts with four words: "I was wrong. Forgive me." Avoid the "if" apology ("I'm sorry *if* you were offended"). Own your part.

A Moment for Reflection

Is there a "gift" you are trying to give to God today while a brother or sister is standing in the back of your mind with a grievance?

You don't have to live with that tension. God is giving you permission — even a command — to step away from the "altar" for a moment to make things right. He will be there when you get back. In fact, He will be more pleased with your "offering" when it is presented by hands that have just been extended in peace.

Closing Prayer

Lord, I thank You for reconciling me to Yourself through the sacrifice of Your Son. I confess that I sometimes try to hide behind religious activities rather than doing the hard work of making peace. Please bring to my mind anyone I have offended. Give me the humility to "go" and the words to say. Let my life be a bridge, not a wall. Amen.

References and Further Reading

- **The Adams-Jefferson Letters:**
  https://www.archives.gov/founding-docs/adams-jefferson-letters

- **Word Study: Diallasso (Reconcile):**
  https://biblehub.com/greek/1259.htm

- **Spurgeon on "The Altar and the Brother":**
  https://www.spurgeon.org/resource-library/sermons/reconciliation/

Reflection

Take a few minutes to reflect and meditate on what you just read. Write down your thoughts take time to pray and praise God.

_____

_____

_____

_____

_____

_____

_____

_____

_____

_____

_____

_____

_____

_____

_____

_____

Day 30

Lay Up
Treasures

"Do not store up for yourselves treasures on earth, where moth and rust destroy, and where thieves break in and steal. But store up for yourselves treasures in heaven, where neither moth nor rust destroys, and where thieves do not break in or steal; for where your treasure is, there your heart will be also.
Matthew 6:19-21

This chapter addresses the ultimate investment strategy. After discussing the horizontal restoration of our relationships, Jesus turns our attention to our vertical priorities regarding our possessions and our passions. He presents a binary choice that determines the security of our future and the orientation of our hearts.

Chapter 30: The Eternal Portfolio

Key Verses: *"Do not store up for yourselves treasures on earth, where moth and rust destroy, and where thieves break in and steal. But store up for yourselves treasures in heaven, where neither moth nor rust destroys, and where thieves do*

not break in or steal; for where your treasure is, there your heart will be also."
— **Matthew 6:19-21 (NASB)**

The Hoarding Instinct

We are natural-born collectors. Whether it is a bank account, a collection of vintage cars, or even digital files, we have an instinct to amass things. In the original Greek, the phrase "store up" is *thesaurizo*, from which we get our word "thesaurus" (a treasury of words). It means to lay up, to hoard, or to accumulate.

Jesus does not condemn the act of storing; He corrects the **location** of the storage. He warns that earthly treasures are subject to "moth and rust." In the ancient world, wealth was often held in expensive fabrics (eaten by moths) or precious metals (corroded by rust).

Even if you manage to preserve the items, "thieves" represent the unpredictable loss of the world—market crashes, inflation, or literal theft. Earthly wealth is an investment in a depreciating asset.

The Transferred Heart

The most profound part of this teaching is the psychological principle in verse 21: **"Where your treasure is, there your heart will be also."** We often think the heart leads the way, but Jesus says the treasure pulls the heart. If you invest your time, money, and energy into your home, your heart will be at home.

If you invest them into your business, your heart will be at the office. If you "lay up" your treasure in the Kingdom of God, your heart will naturally follow. You don't "will" your heart to be heavenly; you move your treasure there, and the heart follows the investment.

A Lesson from History: William Borden's "No Regrets"

William Borden was the heir to the Borden Dairy estate. When he graduated from high school in 1904, he was already a millionaire. He could have spent his life "storing up" earthly treasures in the highest circles of society. Instead, he chose to "lay up" his life and fortune in heaven.

He gave away hundreds of thousands of dollars to missions and set out to be a missionary to Muslims in China. He died of spinal meningitis in Egypt at the age of 25 before he ever reached China.

To the world, his life was a "waste" of treasure. But found in his Bible were three phrases written at different stages of his journey: "No Reserves," "No Retreats," and finally, right before he died, **"No Regrets."** Borden understood that wealth given to God is not lost; it is merely transferred to a more secure account. He didn't lose his life; he invested it.

The Moving Truck Metaphor

There is a common saying: "You've never seen a U-Haul behind a hearse." We cannot take our earthly houses, cars, or bank statements with us when we pass into eternity. However, the Bible suggests that while we cannot take it *with* us, we can send it *ahead*.

Imagine you are moving to a new country. You are currently living in a temporary hotel, but you are sending your furniture, your money, and your valuables to your permanent home across the ocean. You wouldn't spend all your money decorating a hotel room you are leaving tomorrow. You would save it for where you are going to live forever. Laying up treasure in heaven is the act of "sending it ahead."

Wisdom from a "Man of Industry"

Benjamin Franklin, whom we have looked to for his practical wisdom (Chapter 14), had a very clear-eyed view of wealth. While he was successful, he viewed money as a means to an end — specifically the "good works" we discussed in Chapter 13.

Franklin once remarked:

"Wealth is not his that has it, but his that enjoys it."

For the believer, "enjoying" wealth means using it for the purpose it was given: to bless others and advance the Kingdom. Franklin realized that hoarding was a form of bondage, while "laying up" treasure through service was a form of freedom.

How to "Lay Up Treasures" Today

This is not just about writing a check; it is about a lifestyle of eternal investment.

1. **The "Inventory" Check:** Look at your bank statement and your calendar from the last month. Do they show an investment in things that will last (people, the Gospel, kindness) or things that will "rust"?

2. **The "Send it Ahead" Habit:** Look for one way this week to use your resources for someone who can never pay you back. This is the purest form of heavenly investment.

3. **The Heart Check:** When you feel anxious about your finances, remind yourself: "My real treasure is in a place where thieves cannot break in." Shift your focus from your earthly "hotel" to your heavenly "home."

In the Kingdom, your wealth is only truly "treasure" when it is being put to work for the King.

A Moment for Reflection

If you were to lose everything you own today—your house, your accounts, your possessions—how much "treasure" would you have left in heaven?

Don't spend your life building a magnificent sandcastle right at the water's edge. The tide of eternity is coming. Instead, take the "sand" of your life and use it to build something that the "rust" of time cannot touch. Your heart is waiting to be heavenly; you just have to give it a reason to go there.

Closing Prayer

Lord, I confess that I often act as if this world is my permanent home. I spend so much energy protecting my earthly treasures and so little time investing in Your Kingdom. Please help me to loosen my grip on the things that are passing away. Teach me how to "send it ahead" through generosity, service, and love. May my heart be where my Savior is. Amen.

References and Further Reading

- **The Life of William Borden:** https://www.wheaton.edu/about-wheaton/history/william-whiting-borden/

- **Word Study: Thesaurizo (Store Up):** https://biblehub.com/greek/2343.htm

- **Spurgeon on "Treasures in Heaven":** https://www.spurgeon.org/resource-library/sermons/treasures-in-heaven/

- **Benjamin Franklin's "The Way to Wealth":** https://www.gutenberg.org/files/2123/2123-h/2123-h.htm

Reflection

Take a few minutes to reflect and meditate on what you just read. Write down your thoughts take time to pray and praise God.

_____

_____

_____

_____

_____

_____

_____

_____

_____

_____

_____

_____

_____

_____

_____

_____

_____

Day 31

Make Disciples

Go therefore and make disciples of all the nations, baptizing them in the name of the Father and the Son and the Holy Spirit,
Matthew 28:19

This chapter addresses the final marching orders of Jesus Christ. Having navigated the internal disciplines of prayer, repentance, and eternal investment, we now come to the outward mission that justifies our stay on this earth. Jesus does not leave His followers wondering what to do with their remaining time; He gives them a clear, reproductive mandate.

Chapter 31: The Multiplication Mandate

Key Verse: *"Go therefore and make disciples of all the nations, baptizing them in the name of the Father and the Son and the Holy Spirit."* — **Matthew 28:19 (NASB)**

The Command to Reproduce

The "Great Commission" contains only one primary command in the original Greek. While we often focus on the word "Go," the actual imperative verb is **"make disciples"** (*matheteuo*). The word "go" is a participle that is better translated as "as you are going." Jesus is saying that as you move through your life—in your workplace, your neighborhood, and your travels—your primary objective is to make disciples.

A disciple is not merely a student who knows what the teacher knows; a disciple is an apprentice who becomes who the teacher is. To "make a disciple" means to walk alongside someone else until they are capable of walking with Christ on their own. It is the transition from being a consumer of the Gospel to being a producer of the Kingdom.

A Lesson from History: William Carey's "Enquiry"

William Carey, often called the "Father of Modern Missions," lived out Matthew 28:19 with a tenacity that defined "finishing well." In the late 1700s, many in the church believed that the Great Commission was only for the original apostles. Carey challenged this "spiritual laziness" by publishing a groundbreaking pamphlet and eventually setting sail for India.

Carey spent seven years in India before seeing his first convert. He faced the death of his child, the mental breakdown of his wife, and the destruction of years of translation work in a warehouse fire. Yet, he continued to "make disciples." He understood that he wasn't just there to count "decisions," but to build a foundation of believers who could then reach their own people.

His motto remains a challenge to every believer today:

"Expect great things from God; attempt great things for God."

Carey finished well because he realized his life was not his own; it was a tool for the multiplication of the image of God in others.

The Chain of Discipleship

Discipleship is a relay race. No matter how fast you run, if you don't pass the baton to the next runner, the race is lost. Paul described this process to Timothy (whom we met in Chapter 12) when he said, "The things which you have heard from me... entrust these to faithful men who will be able to teach others also" (**2 Timothy 2:2**).

Notice the four generations in that one verse:

1. Paul

2. Timothy

3. Faithful men

4. Others also.

If any one person in that chain had decided to be a "consumer" rather than a "maker of disciples," the Gospel would have stopped with them. Finishing well means ensuring that the fire of faith continues to burn long after your own "lamp" (Chapter 13) has gone out.

Wisdom from the "Navigator"

Dawson Trotman, the founder of The Navigators, was a man obsessed with the idea of "spiritual reproduction." He realized that if one person reached one person for Christ each year and truly discipled them, and then those two each reached one the next year, the entire world could be reached in a single generation.

Trotman famously asked:

"Where is your man? Where is your woman?"

He believed that every Christian should be able to point to at least one other person and say, "I am helping that person grow in Christ." He taught that we aren't called to build big buildings or big programs, but to build big people.

How to "Make Disciples" Today

Making disciples sounds intimidating, but it is actually a very natural process of sharing your life.

1. **Identify Your "Timothy":** Look around your current circle. Is there someone a few steps behind you in their faith journey? Ask God for the courage to invite them to coffee or a regular Bible study.

2. **The "Show and Tell" Method:** Discipleship isn't a classroom lecture; it's an apprenticeship. Invite someone to watch how you "order your prayer" (Chapter 19), how you "render to Caesar" (Chapter 18), or how you handle a conflict (Chapter 22).

3. **The Graduation Goal:** The goal of a disciple-maker is to work themselves out of a job. Your aim is to see your "Timothy" start making their own disciples.

A Moment for Reflection

Are you a "dead end" for the Gospel? You may have "continued in the Word" (Chapter 17) and "laid up treasures" (Chapter 23), but if you aren't passing it on, you are missing the final command of your King.

You don't have to be a theologian to make a disciple. You just have to be a few steps ahead and willing to turn around and offer a hand. Who is following you today? If nobody is following you, are you truly following Him? Today, ask the Lord to give you one person you can invest in.

Closing Prayer

Lord, I thank You that someone was faithful enough to share the Gospel with me. I confess that I've often been content to be a student without ever becoming a teacher. Please give me the heart of a disciple-maker. Show me the person You want me to invest in, and give me the patience and wisdom to walk alongside them. May my life result in a harvest that continues long after I am gone. Amen.

References and Further Reading

- **The Life of William Carey:**
  https://www.christianitytoday.com/history/people/missionaries/william-carey.html

- **Dawson Trotman's "Born to Reproduce":**
  https://www.navigators.org/resource/born-to-reproduce/

- **Word Study: Matheteuo (Make Disciples):**
  https://biblehub.com/greek/3100.htm

Reflection

Take a few minutes to reflect and meditate on what you just read. Write down your thoughts take time to pray and praise God.

_____

_____

_____

_____

_____

_____

_____

_____

_____

_____

_____

_____

_____

_____

_____

_____

_____

_____

Epilogue

Epilogue: Beyond the 31st Day

The book you hold in your hands is not a destination; it is a training manual. If you have reached this page, you have successfully completed a 31-day "Basic Training" in the discipline of the spirit. But as any soldier or athlete will tell you, the purpose of training is not the training itself—it is the battle and the race that follow.

The Myth of the "Finished" Habit

There is a common misconception that once a habit is formed, it becomes effortless. In the spiritual life, this is a dangerous myth. The "flesh" (Chapter 31) does not stop looking for supply lines, and the "speculations" (Chapter 30) do not stop knocking at the gate.

To "finish well" is not to reach a point where you no longer need to try; it is to reach a point where your first instinct is to turn to God. The goal of the **Command Habit** is to make obedience your default setting.

The Legacy of the Persistent

Throughout this journey, we have walked with giants like **William Tyndale**, who translated until his last breath, and **Fanny Crosby**, who sang through her darkness. They didn't finish well because they were superhuman; they finished well because they were *consistent*. They understood that the secret to a great life is a thousand small, "commanded" moments stacked on top of one another.

As you close this book and step into Day 32 and beyond, remember the words of the educator Horace Mann:

"Be ashamed to die until you have won some victory for humanity."

Your greatest victory will not be a singular event. It will be the daily victory of a mind that is captured, a heart that is thankful, and a soul that abides.

Your Final Charge

Don't let the "Command Habit" become a memory of a month-long experiment. Let it be the architecture of your life.

- When the world is loud, **abide**.

- When the heart is heavy, **rejoice**.

- When the path is dark, **pray**.

You have the tools. You have the Word. You have the Savior. Now, go and live the truth — and let that truth make you truly free.

Grace and peace to you as you finish well.

Final Reflection

Which of these 31 days challenged you the most? That is likely the area where your "Command Habit" needs the most ongoing attention. Return to that chapter often. The Word of God is a well that never runs dry.

Summary

This "Master Map" provides a comprehensive overview of your 31-day journey in **The Command Habit**.

Part 1: The Great Commandments

Day 1: Love God

- **Key Verse:** *"You shall love the Lord your God with all your heart and with all your soul and with all your might."* — **Deuteronomy 6:5**

- **Summary:** Establish the "Vertical Priority." True discipleship begins by ordering your "muchness"—your time, talents, and resources—around the supremacy of God.

- **Key Points:**

  o God is the "True North" for every decision.

  o Love is a decisive act of the will, not just an emotion.

  o Our "muchness" (abundance) belongs to the Creator.

Day 2: Love Others

- **Key Verse:** *"The second is this, 'You shall love your neighbor as yourself.'"* — **Mark 12:31**

- **Summary:** The "Horizontal Reflex." Our love for God is proven by how we treat the "neighbor" (the one who is near).

- **Key Points:**

  o Love is the evidence of a transformed heart.

  o Treating others as "Image-Bearers" of God.

  o Service is love in work clothes

Part 2: The Atmosphere of the Soul

Day 3: Rejoice Always

- **Key Verse:** *"Rejoice always."* — **1 Thessalonians 5:16**

- **Summary:** Choosing joy as a spiritual discipline rather than an emotional reaction to circumstances.

- **Key Points:**

  o The "Thermostat" vs. "Thermometer" mentality.

  o Joy is rooted in the character of God, which never changes.

  o Rejoicing "evicts" bitterness from the mind.

Day 4: Pray Without Ceasing

- **Key Verse:** *"Pray without ceasing."* — **1 Thessalonians 5:17**

- **Summary:** Maintaining a "live connection" with the Father through every mundane and monumental moment of the day.

- **Key Points:**

  o Prayer as "Spiritual Breathing."

  o Living in the constant awareness of God's presence.

  o Turning every task into a conversation with the Divine.

Day 5: In All Things Give Thanks

- **Key Verse:** *"In everything give thanks; for this is the will of God..."* — **1 Thessalonians 5:18**

- **Summary:** Developing the "Grace Filter" to find God's goodness even in difficult seasons or "flea-infested" circumstances.

- **Key Points:**

  o Giving thanks *in* everything, not necessarily *for* everything.

- o   Gratitude acts as a spiritual greenhouse for the soul.

- o   The "But God" reframe for negative situations.

Part 3: The Internal Fortress

Day 6: Take Every Thought Captive

- **Key Verse:** *"We are taking every thought captive to the obedience of Christ."* — **2 Corinthians 10:5**

- **Summary:** Engaging in the battle for the mind by arresting rogue thoughts and speculations before they become strongholds.

- **Key Points:**

    - o   Leading thoughts away "at spearpoint."

    - o   Replacing "what ifs" with the "He is" of Scripture.

    - o   The 10-second rule for mental gatekeeping.

Day 7: Make No Provision For The Flesh

- **Key Verse:** *"Put on the Lord Jesus Christ, and make no provision for the flesh..."* — **Romans 13:14**

- **Summary:** Starving the enemy by cutting the supply lines to our old nature and old habits.

- **Key Points:**

    - o   Temptation requires "logistics"; stop packing for the trip.

    - o   "Putting on" Christ leaves no room for the baggage of the world.

    - o   Preventative discipline: deciding the win before the battle begins.

Part 4: The Micah Mandate & Mindset

Day 8: Seek Justice

- **Key Verse:** *"What does the Lord require of you... but to do justice?"* — **Micah 6:8a**

- **Summary:** Active righteousness. The believer is called to align their life with God's standard of equity and fairness in the world.

- **Key Points:**

  o Justice is love in a social context.

  o Protecting the vulnerable as an act of worship.

Day 9: Love Mercy

- **Key Verse:** *"...to love kindness [mercy]..."* — **Micah 6:8b**

- **Summary:** Mirroring God's *hesed* (steadfast love). We don't just "do" mercy; we learn to cherish the opportunity to show it.

- **Key Points:**

  o Mercy is not getting what we deserve; grace is getting what we don't.

  o Letting go of "the right to get even."

Day 10: Walk Humbly with God

- **Key Verse:** *"...and to walk humbly with your God."* — **Micah 6:8c**

- **Summary:** The posture of the pilgrim. Realizing that we are small, He is great, and the privilege is simply being near Him.

- **Key Points:**

  o Humility is not thinking less of yourself, but thinking of yourself less.

  o Keeping in step with the Spirit's pace.

Day 11: What you Dwell Upon

- **Key Verse:** *"Whatever is true... honorable... right... dwell on these things."* — **Philippians 4:8**

- **Summary:** Intentional focus. Our character is the "sum total" of our persistent thoughts.

- **Key Points:**

   o The "Mental Garden": pull the weeds, water the truth.

   o High-quality thoughts lead to high-quality living.

Day 12: Set Your Mind

- **Key Verse:** *"Set your mind on the things above, not on the things that are on earth."* — **Colossians 3:2**

- **Summary:** Directional thinking. We must "fix our eyes" on the eternal to survive the temporary.

- **Key Points:**

   o The "Compass" habit: re-centering daily on heaven's perspective.

   o Earthly things are tools; heavenly things are treasures.

Part 5: The Daily Discipline of Trust

Day 13: Draw Near to God/Abide

- **Key Verse:** *"Draw near to God and He will draw near to you."* — **James 4:8**

- **Summary:** Proactive intimacy. God is a rewarder of those who diligently seek Him.

- **Key Points:**

    o The "Meno" habit: staying in the vine to produce fruit.

    o Drawing near requires clearing the "clutter" between us and God.

Day 14: Commit Your Works

- **Key Verse:** *"Commit your works to the Lord and your plans will be established."* — **Proverbs 16:3**

- **Summary:** Strategic surrender. Turning over the "output" of our labor to the one who provides the "input."

- **Key Points:**

    o Working for an "Audience of One."

    o Trusting the process when the results are hidden.

Day 15: Do Not Become Conformed

- **Key Verse:** *"And do not be conformed to this world, but be transformed..."* — **Romans 12:2**

- **Summary:** Resisting the "Mold." The world tries to squeeze us into its shape; the Spirit transforms us from the inside out.

- **Key Points:**

    o The "Non-Conformist" habit: questioning the cultural "default."

- o Renewing the mind through the constant wash of the Word.

Day 16: Trust in the Lord

- **Key Verse:** *"Trust in the Lord with all your heart and do not lean on your own understanding."* — **Proverbs 3:5-6**

- **Summary:** Abandoning self-sufficiency. Trusting God's character when His "map" doesn't make sense to us.

- **Key Points:**

  - o The "Leaning" test: what are you propping your life up on?

  - o Acknowledge Him in *all* ways — even the small ones.

Day 17: Be Strong and Courageous

- **Key Verse:** *"Have I not commanded you? Be strong and courageous!"* — **Joshua 1:9**

- **Summary:** Commanded bravery. Courage is not the absence of fear, but the presence of God.

- **Key Points:**

  - o God's presence is the "fuel" for our strength.

  - o Acting in faith despite how we feel.

Part 6: Navigating the World's Snares

Day 18: Keep Free from Love of Money

- **Key Verse:** *"Make sure that your character is free from the love of money..."* — **Hebrews 13:5**

- **Summary:** Financial freedom. Ensuring that money is a servant and never a master.

- **Key Points:**

    o   Contentment is the cure for the "Always More" disease.

    o   Trusting in the Provider over the Provision.

Day 19: Flee Temptation

- **Key Verse:** *"Now flee from youthful lusts and pursue righteousness..."* — **2 Timothy 2:22**

- **Summary:** The "Joseph" habit. Sometimes the most courageous thing you can do is run away.

- **Key Points:**

    o   Identify the "exit ramp" God provides in every trial.

    o   Fleeing the bad *requires* pursuing the good simultaneously.

Day 20: Shine Your Light

- **Key Verse:** *"Let your light shine before men in such a way that they may see your good works..."* — **Matthew 5:16**

- **Summary:** Visible faith. Our "Command Habits" are not just for us; they are lanterns for others.

- **Key Points:**

    o   Your character is a "silent sermon" to a watching world.

    o   Giving the glory back to the Father.

Day 21: Cast Your Burden

- **Key Verse:** *"Cast your burden upon the Lord and He will sustain you."* — **Psalm 55:22**

- **Summary:** Relinquishing weight. We were not built to carry the "pack" of worry; we were built to carry the "yoke" of Christ.

- **Key Points:**

    o   The "Exchange" habit: giving God the weight, receiving His strength.

    o   Sustainability comes from God's shoulders, not ours.

Part 7: The Final Stretch — Living the Kingdom

Day 22: Love One Another

- **Key Verse:** *"A new commandment I give to you, that you love one another..."* — **John 13:34**

- **Summary:** The Family Mark. The distinguishing characteristic of the Church is a radical, sacrificial love.

- **Key Points:**

    o   Loving "as He loved": the cross as our standard.

Day 23: Choose Who You will Serve

- **Key Verse:** *"Choose for yourselves today whom you will serve... as for me and my house, we will serve the Lord."* — **Joshua 24:15**

- **Summary:** The Daily Choice. Every morning is a "re-election" of the Lord as King of your day.

- **Key Points:**

  o Ambivalence is a choice for the enemy.

  o The "House" habit: leading by example in your closest circles.

Day 24: Continue in God's Word

- **Key Verse:** *"If you continue in My word, then you are truly disciples of Mine..."* — **John 8:31-32**

- **Summary:** The "Meno" habit of residence. Staying with the truth until it becomes a part of your DNA.

- **Key Points:**

  o Discipleship is an apprenticeship, not a course.

  o Truth found in continuity leads to freedom.

Day 25: Render to Caesar

- **Key Verse:** *"Render to Caesar the things that are Caesar's; and to God the things that are God's."* — **Matthew 22:21**

- **Summary:** Dual citizenship. Living as faithful citizens of earth while prioritizing our ultimate citizenship in heaven.

- **Key Points:**

  o Integrity in our civic and financial duties.

  o The "Image" test: we carry God's image, so we belong to Him.

Day 26: Watch and Pray

- **Key Verse:** *"Keep watching and praying that you may not come into temptation..."* — **Matthew 26:41**

- **Summary:** Vigilant Readiness. Recognizing the spirit is willing, but the flesh is weak.

- **Key Points:**

    o The "Sentry" habit: staying awake to spiritual dangers.

Day 27: Repent

- **Key Verse:** *"Repent, for the kingdom of heaven is at hand."* — **Matthew 4:17**

- **Summary:** The Course Correction. Repentance is not just being sorry; it's a 180-degree change of direction.

- **Key Points:**

    o "Turning toward the Light."

    o Daily repentance keeps the heart soft.

Day 28: Love Your Enemies

- **Key Verse:** *"But I say to you, love your enemies and pray for those who persecute you."* — **Matthew 5:44**

- **Summary:** The Impossible Love. Breaking the cycle of hate with the "supernatural" habit of kindness.

- **Key Points:**

    o Prayer as the first step in loving an enemy.

Day 29: Be Reconciled

- **Key Verse:** *"First be reconciled to your brother, and then come and present your offering."* — **Matthew 5:24**

- **Summary:** Relationship priority. God values our horizontal peace as much as our vertical worship.

- **Key Points:**

    o The "Short Accounts" habit: don't let the sun go down on a grudge.

Day 30: Lay-up Treasures

- **Key Verse:** *"Store up for yourselves treasures in heaven... for where your treasure is, there your heart will be also."* — **Matthew 6:19-21**

- **Summary:** Eternal investment. Investing our lives in things that "rust" cannot touch and "thieves" cannot steal.

- **Key Points:**

  o Moving your "treasure" moves your "heart."

Day 31: Make Disciples

- **Key Verse:** *"Go therefore and make disciples of all the nations..."* — **Matthew 28:19**

- **Summary:** The Great Commission Finish. Our habits are meant to be contagious—finishing well means helping others start well.

- **Key Points:**

  o Every disciple is called to be a "multiplier."

  o The "Finish Well" habit: finishing the work God gave us to do.

Final Thoughts

First, thank you so much for taking the time to read this book. It is my prayer that this has been a blessing to you and your family.

Secondly, if you have an opportunity to send me an e-mail with your thoughts, comments or suggestions, that would be very helpful.

Finally, I hope you were encouraged and strengthened by what you read.

paulbeersdorf@gmail.com

Blessings to you and your family!

Paul Beersdorf